TALES from the GRAND CANYON

The author (fourth from front) and friend Orpha Ochse (third from front) begin their descent into the canyon in 1953.

TALES from the GRAND CANYON

SOME TRUE, SOME TALL

by Edna Evans

Northland Press  Flagstaff, Arizona

Frontispiece: Tourists guided down the Bright Angel Trail, 1953

CONTENTS

Grand Canyon vista including Bright Angel Trail, Indian Gardens Camp, and Plateau Point.

INTRODUCTION

"WHAT TIME DO THE LIGHTS GO ON IN THE CANYON?" "IS THERE AN ELEVATOR TO the bottom?" "Where is the sunset? I heard it was at Desert View." "Why did they build the canyon so close to the hotel?" These are some of the many questions asked on either rim of the canyon every year. To people who know the canyon—rangers, park employees, many-time visitors—the questions are funny. To newcomers they are not.

The Grand Canyon is not funny. Neither is the Colorado River. It would be as hard to laugh at or about them as it would be to laugh at an earthquake, joke about the Pyramids, or poke fun at the Ten Commandments. But funny things can and do happen at the canyon, and people visiting or living in the area do and say ridiculous things. Mainly, it is the visitors who are on the receiving end of the jokes, puns, and amusing stories.

There seems to be an overall pattern to Grand Canyon humor with variations that depend on who tells the story and whom or what the story is about. Some of the humor is gentle, calling for a smile; some a little less kind calls for a snort or snicker; a few deserve a deep belly, roll-'em-in-the-aisles kind of laugh. There are dumb tourist jokes, mule trail jokes, tall tales told by rangers, bus drivers, and tour leaders, and then there are some that belong in a class by themselves.

One of the people to describe creation of the canyon in a funny way was the

Arizona humorist Dick Wick Hall. Dick lived in Salome (where she danced), sold laughing gas to tourists, and wrote for the *Saturday Evening Post*. He is the creator of the Desert Frog, which was seven years old, lived under the garage, cried dusty tears, and never learned to swim. He also had a liking for capital letters; according to Dick, B.C. stands for the time of the Big Crawfish, and A.D. stands for All Dry—only in Arizona, of course. He said it happened this way:

> Arizona at one time was All Under Water Two or Three Thousand Feet Deep. Now the Water is about All Two or Three Thousand Feet Deep Under Arizona which is pretty good Proof that some time or other we turned Bottom Side Up. The Whole World must have been Pretty Sick on the Day Arizona was Born, and it Heaved and Twisted around and Groaned a Lot—and What it finally Poked up through the Ocean is Now called Arizona. From the looks of things around here Now, Arizona must have got Treated Pretty Rough on its Birth Day, ten or 20,000,000 Years ago, and some Awful Scars are left on it even now, the best Known of which is called the Grand Canyon.

Some visitors know very little about the canyon and its history, as is illustrated by the story of the three young women from the East who photographed each other standing in front of the Powell Monument at Hopi Point. Powell, they decided, had "discovered" the Grand Canyon.

"But I heard that some Spaniards discovered it," one objected, "and Powell isn't a Spanish name." They laughed at that and then read the inscription on the monument. "Oh, they went through in boats," another commented. "Boats, in this country?" "Not up here on the rim," the first one said. "They went through down below." "Oh," said the third one who had been silent up to then. "Is there a river at the bottom?"

There are a number of stories about religious fundamentalists who are shocked by geological lectures about the canyon's age. One visitor complained that the park service was blasphemous and should be punished. She (the story says it was a female visitor who objected) even wrote to Washington, protesting about the lecture on canyon geology given daily at Yavapai Point. The Bible, she said, told of how the world was six thousand years old and had been created in six days. And what right, she wanted to know, did the park service have to contradict the Bible?

There is the story about a famous engineer who walked to the rim and inquired about the depth, the width, and the length of the canyon. After getting the information, he gazed at the view for a time and then said, "Well, it's a hell of a big hole, but what do you bet that I can't fill it up for a dollar a cubic yard?"

Sometimes a ranger is hard put to keep a straight face when a tourist wants to know how far below sea level the Colorado River is. Just how the river could flow uphill before reaching the Gulf of California is more than his scientific training can explain.

And one final tourist yarn is about the ranger who overheard a woman pointing out to her companions a dry wash in a side canyon. She told them it was the Colorado River. The ranger stepped up politely and said, "I beg your pardon, ma'am, but that is Trinity Wash, and it is dry at this time of the year. The Colorado River is not visible at this point." The woman drew herself up haughtily. "I know better," she declared. "My cousin was here three years ago and he said he could see the river from here. I will take my cousin's word for it anytime to that of a perfect stranger!"

The mule trains that go down the trail every day, carrying nervous tourists into the canyon and back, are the source of many humorous stories. The mules, of course, are four-footed elevators. The wranglers who look after the mules try to dress, act, and talk the part of the Old West. At the same time, they have to reassure any frightened riders and keep the whole string of riders and animals safe. According to regulations, no rider can weigh more than two hundred pounds, but the wranglers say that some of the larger people lie about their weight. Lifting them onto a mule and off again causes many hernias, the "occupational disease" of the wranglers. As for the mules, they say there is one named Dopey who deserves retirement to green and peaceful pastures because he has carried so many "heavies" down the trail.

It is wise not to ask a wrangler whether people get killed very often on the canyon rides. His answer is liable to be, "No, ma'am, only once."

For the timid rider who asks for a gentle mule, the wrangler has a standard reply. "Well, ma'am," he says solemnly, "I'm right sorry but we just sent the last gentle mule down with another party. But if you ain't never rode before, why we'll just give you a mule that ain't never been rode, neither. That way you can both start right out together." He may add for further reassurance, "Just you hang on to that saddle horn, lady. Just hang right on to it, an' pull hard. If you pull it off, just hand it to me an' I'll put it back on for you."

For the rider who asks about chances of falling off the trail, there is this comforting advice. "If you fall off, sir, be sure to keep your eyes open. They tell me the scenery is awful purty on the way down."

For several years after a famous writer described a ride into the canyon aboard a mule named Napoleon, many visitors wanted to ride that particular animal.

"Where's Napoleon?" they would ask. "That's him," the wrangler answered, pointing to the nearest mule. And that is why, for some time, Napoleon was the name of every mule in the park. Sometimes Napoleon was white or brown, sometimes male and frequently female. It didn't matter—just so the visitor was riding Napoleon.

In the Fred Harvey Company files are three rather unusual letters, the first from a woman complaining about the mules she and her husband rode on the trail to Phantom Ranch. "I do not pretend to be an authority of the proper conditions for healthy mules," she wrote, "but it seemed to me inhumane to see these beasts as they are. The appearance is noticed first. Rough, shaggy, and dirty coats. Their hair is in need of being brushed as it kept coming off over everything. Some had manure stains and some had sores and scars of past sores—indicating misuse or mistreatment. Upon inquiry I was led to understand that the proper feed for this type of animal is grass—they are getting green hay. While riding behind other mules it is quite unpleasant because of the gas that is passed along the way. It would seem to me that all these conditions would shorten the lives of these animals and in some cases endanger the riders. I am inquiring further to find if Arizona has a Humane Society, and if I find one I intend informing them of these same conditions."

To this letter, the company's transportation operating manager wrote in reply: "The mules are shaggy looking as they have not shed all of their winter coat, and it will be the early part of June before they are sleek looking. However, there is no excuse for them to be dirty looking, and I can assure you that they are brushed clean, especially underneath the saddle every day. None of our mules, when used, have sore backs. . . . Our mules get the best food money can buy . . . and we welcome the humane society or the National Park Service to inspect our stock at any time."

A copy of these letters went to Dagget Harvey in the main office, and Mr. Harvey in turn wrote to the manager. "I think your reply to Mrs.——'s letter about the condition of our mules is excellent—both tactful and lucid. However, you neglected to answer one of her complaints. She makes this comment: 'While riding behind other mules it is quite unpleasant because of the gas that is passed along the way.' Don't you think it would have been true Fred Harvey service if we had assured her that, from now on, all of our mules would be corked while they are making the trail trips? Of course, this might have a ballooning effect on the mules and perhaps we could introduce a new service: Take a Muleycopter to the bottom of the Canyon"!

Bus drivers and tour leaders have their own bag of jokes, too. At Pima Point, for example, where the drop is a sheer thousand feet, the bus driver likes to tell of the lady who fell over the edge here but landed unhurt. Why? Very simple; she was wearing light fall clothing.

Another place, with sheer walls straight down, is called Poison Point, the driver explains. It is called that for a good reason: one drop kills you.

The tour leader on a trip to Phantom Ranch assures everyone that the suspension bridge across the Colorado is safe. It is guaranteed to hold ninety tons—one at a time.

The park, everyone is informed at some time or other, is the third largest in the lower forty-eight states. As of 1983, it contained 1,218,375 square acres—most of them standing on edge.

A favorite yarn at campfire programs is supposed to be a personal experience of the ranger telling it. Once, while on patrol in a remote part of the canyon, the ranger ran out of food and he had only one bullet left in his gun (the gun was for protection, of course, to be used only in an emergency).

This was an emergency, so the ranger hunted until he found two quail sitting close together in a bush. Taking careful aim, he fired and hit both quail with one bullet. But when he picked them up, he found he had killed six more quail on the other side of the bush.

The shot frightened a big buck mule deer that ran into a nearby pond and got bogged down in the mud. The ranger dropped the quail and ran to get the deer, and in carrying it out he sank down over his boot tops in the water. Reaching shore, he pulled off his boots to pour out the water and he found in them a dozen nice fish. Placing the quail, the deer, and the fish together to carry to his camp, he was struggling to get the load on his shoulders. This put a great strain on his suspender buttons and one button flew off with such force that it killed a rabbit hopping along fifty yards behind him.

Big country inspires big stories and over the years the Grand Canyon has inspired its share of stories. Some of them are true and some are tall tales told to entertain, impress, or astound the thousands of people who come each year from all parts of the world to see the canyon.

Some of the true tales sound like whoppers; some of the tall stories seem perfectly logical. It is hard to believe that one can stand on the canyon rim and look down at layers of earth's history, beginning with topsoil that is geologically young, and continuing with deeper layers that are more than two billion years old. In those colorful layers are records of ancient seas, of deserts and swamplands, as well as the fossils and footprints of creatures that lived and died millions of years ago. It is equally hard to believe that the Colorado River has been patiently at work in the canyon for ten million years, yet these are details of a true story.

On the other hand, it is equally as difficult to believe the Arizona rancher's account of what happened when he tried to get rid of a pesky prairie dog that was raiding his kitchen garden. When he saw the critter disappear into a hole, the rancher decided to dig it out. He began digging and so did the prairie dog. Both kept on until they hit bedrock and the man finally caught the varmint; then he looked up and discovered that he had dug the Grand Canyon. Now that is a tall tale.

The dividing line between a true tale and a tall one is sometimes hard to determine; often it depends on the experience of the hearer. To the Indians of a hundred and fifty years ago, stories about wagons that could go without horses to pull them (locomotives) were unbelievable. To city dwellers today, cooking with hot rocks in a basket or chopping down a tree with a stone axe seems equally impossible. The geological story of the Grand Canyon is hard to believe and so are many of the historical events that have taken place on its rims and within its massive walls. It is those contrasts that have inspired this book.

The chapters that follow tell tales about the canyon from early times to the present. Ranging from Indian legends to wild yarns to survey records, the tales, it is hoped, will make knowing about the great gorge a more enjoyable experience.

According to Indian legend, the daughter of this Havasupai waterfall became a parent to the human race.

CHAPTER I

A HISTORY TALE

PEOPLE HAVE BEEN VISITING THE GRAND CANYON FOR ABOUT FOURTEEN THOUSAND years, according to archaeologists. Throughout those centuries, there probably were many canyon stories told, but until recently there was no way to keep them from fading out of human memory. What the early canyon visitors thought and said is lost forever, but it should be no surprise that all five of the Indian tribes who live in the Grand Canyon area today have legends about it.

The Havasupai Indians, who live in a lovely side canyon west of the national park area, have a flood story to explain the big canyon. In the beginning, so the story goes, there were two gods of the universe: Tochopa, a good god, and Hokomatka, an evil god. As could be expected, the two gods quarreled, and the evil one said he was going to drown the world. In order to save his beautiful daughter, Tochopa hollowed out a piñon log, stocked it with plenty of supplies, and put his daughter inside.

The rains came and flooded the earth, but the log floated and protected the girl. Finally the storm ended and the flood waters ran off into the sea, cutting the Grand Canyon as they went. The girl climbed out of her log and settled down to weave some baskets. When the sun came out to drive away the darkness, the girl fell in love with him. He liked her, too, and soon they had a son. But the warm sun was not a very satisfactory husband, and later the girl had an affair with one of the waterfalls in Havasu Canyon. This time she had a daughter. When the two

9

children grew up they were married and became the parents of the whole human race.

The Havasupais also have a story about the two tall red sandstone spires that stand at the entrance to their canyon. The two were once a Havasupai chief and his wife, and for some reason, they decided to pack up and leave the canyon. Tochopa did not want his people to go, so he turned the chief and his wife into stone just as they were starting up the trail that leads out of the canyon. There they still stand as a warning to other possible migrants.

As long as those two sandstone columns remain standing, the Indians say, all will be well in Havasu Canyon. If one or both should ever fall, that would mean the end of the Havasupais and their canyon home. Fortunately, the two sandstone pillars are good solid rock and will probably last for several thousand years.

The Walapais, who are related to the Havasupais, also have a how-the-canyon-was-made legend. According to them, long ago a great flood covered the earth with water so that nothing alive could stir. Their culture hero, Pack-i-tha-a-wi, made a big knife out of flint and waded out into the flood carrying the knife in one hand and a heavy wooden club in the other. He stuck the knife into the water-covered ground and pounded it deeper with the club. He kept on pounding and moving the knife back and forth until he formed the Grand Canyon through which the flood waters rushed out into the Sea of the Sunset; then the sun shone and the ground became hard and dry, the way it is today.

The Navajos, whose twenty-five thousand square miles of reservation border Grand Canyon National Park on the east, believe that a great inland sea once covered the whole area. Waves of the sea washed against the shore and finally opened up a passageway across the land. The water rushed away, the sea drained dry, and the channel it left behind became the Grand Canyon. In order to keep from being drowned in the flood, many of the Navajos' ancestors turned themselves into fish. For this reason, no good Navajo likes to go fishing or wants to eat fish for fear of harming a relative.

The Paiutes, who live north of the canyon, also have a flood story, one which they told to Major John Wesley Powell when he was exploring the region. Long ago, the Paiutes say, the wife of one of their great chiefs died and the chief mourned her loss. To comfort him, the god Tavwoats told the chief that his wife had gone to a happier land. "I will take you to the Spirit Land and you can see how happy she is," Tavwoats said. "Then you must not mourn anymore. You must also promise not to travel that trail again as long as you live."

The chief promised, so Tavwoats took his magic ball and rolled it against the mountains, tearing a great gash in them and opening the way to a beautiful land far to the southwest. The chief and Tavwoats followed the trail, and the chief saw that his wife was happy in the Spirit Land. Then he was satisfied.

After they returned home, Tavwoats rolled a great river into the deep trail so that no other living person could travel that way again. The river was the Colorado and the trail was the Grand Canyon.

The Paiutes also told Major Powell other tales. There were strange, weird creatures called Oonupin, they said, that came out of the canyon and hovered around the camp at night. They could be frightened away by loud singing or by firing a gun at them. There were also spirits called Rock Rovers. They built fires at night on remote high places in the canyon and tried to lure human beings away from home. This explained what happened when someone disappeared in the canyon mazes and was never heard from again.

The Hopi Indians believe that their ancestors came up from the World Below through a hole in the earth, which they call the Sipapu. That opening, or Place of Emergence, is located in the Grand Canyon about ninety miles west of the village of Oraibi. Where else than in the Grand Canyon could a Hopi be closer to the World Below?

For generations, the Hopis made annual pilgrimages from their mesa-top villages down into the canyon to gather salt from seepages along the Colorado River. On the way down, each man would carve his clan symbol on the rocks—a sort of "Kilroy was here" mark—to show he was brave enough to make the trip. This yearly Hopi custom ended when trading posts made salt more readily available on the reservation.

As long as there are people with curiosity and imagination, the creation legends will continue. Many changes have taken place in the ten million years that the Grand Canyon has been in existence; it is a never-ending process. Legends from the past are often forgotten, but others take their places.

In the sixteenth century, tales of the Spanish exploration and "discovery" of the Grand Canyon began to spread. Their tales are not of creation—indeed, they were little concerned with how the canyon got there—but of the hardships endured in trying to circumvent the canyon. To those at home, the canyon tales told by Spanish explorers undoubtedly seemed tall. Yet as they stood on the edge of the great precipice, the Spaniards found it hard to believe their Indian guides who told of a great river at the bottom of the canyon.

These early explorers, the first Europeans to stand on the edge of the canyon and look down into its depths, were two dozen Spaniards led by Captain Garcia Lopez de Cardenas. They arrived at the south rim in September of 1540 and were not particularly impressed with what they saw. Captain Cardenas found it hard to believe his Hopi Indian guides who told him that the river at the bottom of the canyon was half a league wide. To Cardenas, standing more than a mile above it, the muddy Colorado looked about six feet across.

The Spanish captain was an officer in the grand exploring expedition led by Francisco Vasquez de Coronado. The Spaniards had come from Mexico to look for the Seven Cities of Cibola—cities built of gold and filled with treasures—that were supposed to exist in what is today the American Southwest. Not wishing to miss any possibilities, Coronado sent out small exploring parties as he went along. Cardenas led one of these and his assignment was to investigate an Indian tale about a great river somewhere in the West. That is how he happened to arrive at the Grand Canyon.

In carrying out his orders, Cardenas and his men spent three days searching for a way from the canyon rim to the river. Water was scarce on the rim, and after their first night out, Captain Cardenas declared that the area was so cold that no one would ever be able to live there. After considerable effort, not even a game trail to the bottom could be found. In the exact words of the captain's report: "The descent was found to be impossible, for at the end of three days Captain Melgosa, with Juan Galeras and another companion, they being the lightest and most agile, undertook to clamber down at a place that appeared to them to be the least difficult. They kept descending in the sight of the men left above until they were lost from view." Cardenas, himself, did not make the climb; he stayed on the rim with the rest of the party.

"At four o'clock in the afternoon," the report continues, "the three returned without having been able to reach the bottom because of the great obstacles they encountered. What from above appeared to be easy proved to be, on the contrary, rough and difficult. They said they had been only a third of the way down, but from the place they reached the river looked very large. Indeed, judging from what they saw, it must be as wide as the Indians had said. The men who remained above estimated that some small rocks jutting from the wall of the Canyon must be about as high as a man. But those who went down swore that when they reached them they were found to be taller than the highest tower in Seville."

It is sad that the names of only two of the agile explorers were mentioned. The third man, who must have climbed as hard as the other two, did not get his name recorded in history. The account is a second-hand story by Pedro de Castenada, who wrote of the whole Coronado expedition twenty years after it was over. Pedro de Sotomayor, who was official reporter for the expedition, was on the first visit to the canyon. But the report he wrote and later gave to the expedition commander has never been found among the Spanish archives. How, when, where, or why the first eyewitness account of the canyon was lost, nobody knows.

Cardenas's discovery of a big gash in a worthless piece of country did not impress Coronado, the Spanish leader. He was looking for treasure, for natives wearing gold jewelry, and for cities where house walls glittered with jewels. He was not interested in scenery, however impressive, or in country where water was scarce and the climate was too cold for comfort. Coronado's expedition marched on, and the Spaniards had no further interest in the Grand Canyon.

For the next three hundred years only two or three explorers saw the canyon. James Ohio Pattie, a trapper from Kentucky, may have seen it in 1826, but the account he wrote was so vague and his tales so tall that no one can tell whether he was on the north rim or the south. A few other mountain men and trappers may have seen it, too, but they just looked and moved on. Nobody bothered to write so much as a word about it.

In 1857, a United States army engineer named Lt. Joseph Christmas Ives was given the job of surveying the Colorado River area, newly acquired from the Mexicans. With the federal government paying the bill, Lieutenant Ives had a small Philadelphia-built steamboat taken apart, packed in crates, and shipped west in order to find out how far up the river a boat could safely go. It was uncrated and put together again on a mud flat at the mouth of the Colorado. Lieutenant Ives called his boat, all fifty-four feet of it, the *Explorer*. In it he and his crew steamed up the Colorado as far as they could: to a place called Black Canyon. Beyond there, the current was too swift and the rocks too big for the little *Explorer,* iron ship though she was. So Lieutenant Ives and his men went ashore and marched overland to explore the western end of the Grand Canyon.

Like Captain Cardenas before him, Lieutenant Ives was not impressed. Considering the way the canyon attracts visitors today, Lieutenant Ives's official report reads like a tall tale. "The region is, of course, altogether valueless," he wrote. "It can be approached only from the south, and after entering it there is nothing to do but leave. It seems intended by nature that the Colorado River, along the greater portion of its lonely and majestic way, shall be forever unvisited and undisturbed." Yet it would be only twelve years until someone would make Lt. Ives's statement completely false.

It was simple enough for a few early explorers to stand at the edge of the canyon and look at the river far below, or for Lt. Ives to explore the calmer, western region of the river and canyon. But what was it like in the deepest recesses of the canyon, and what was happening in all the miles of river that could not be seen? Nobody knew for sure. No one had ever followed the Colorado through the canyon and lived to tell about it. Exploration from the east ended where the canyon began and farther west it began where the canyon ended. What lay between was completely unknown territory.

There were—and still are—many tales about that unexplored waterway. Some said the Colorado River roared over cliffs and created falls as big as Niagara. Others declared that the river disappeared into a cave and flowed underground for miles. Some even said that the Colorado plunged into the center of the earth and never came up again. This one is particularly tall considering the river does emerge from the canyon and flows south to empty into the Gulf of California several hundred miles away. There were steamboats on the lower Colorado to prove it.

The one man who dared to solve the mystery was small in stature but big in courage and scientific curiosity. He also had only one arm, his left one; he had lost his right arm, from just below the elbow, in the Battle of Shiloh during the Civil War. The man was Major John Wesley Powell, a Union army veteran. After the war, he taught geology and natural history for a few years at Illinois State Normal University, but he had one question that no textbook could answer: he wanted to know what happened to the Colorado River as it flowed through the Grand Canyon.

Powell set out to find the answer in the summer of 1869, starting from Green River Station in Wyoming with nine men and four specially built rowboats. His idea was to float down the Green River to where it joined with the Grand to form the Colorado. From there he and his men would go through the Grand Canyon to see what they could see.

A small crowd gathered to see them off, and once out of sight the explorers were out of touch with the world for fourteen weeks. After a month or so they were given up for lost, and nobody ever expected them to come out of the canyon alive.

The trip was a hard one. Even before they reached the Colorado they had lost one boat with its provisions and supplies. They ran through numerous rapids or, when they could, floated the boats through the bad places with lines from shore. They called this "letting the boats down" and it was safer than riding them through the rough water. Every rapid meant getting soaked and drying out men and supplies later. So much water was not good for their food supplies, and before long they were living on nothing more exciting than rancid bacon, soggy coffee, and mildewed flour—and not much of that as the weeks went by.

One man wisely chose to leave the expedition early while there was still time to return to safety. The others continued on, deeper and deeper into the canyon where the rapids were bigger and the food supply grew smaller. Finally, three men decided that the odds against survival looked too great. They elected to leave the expedition and climb out of the canyon, hoping to make their way overland and back to civilization. The place where they left is called Separation Point.

Two days later, Powell and the rest of his expedition—six men in the two remaining boats—floated out of the canyon. The first human beings they saw were three white men and an Indian who were fishing in the river and keeping an eye out for any wreckage from the lost expedition that might be drifting down with the current. Powell had reached the mouth of the Virgin River; he had made it through the canyon.

As for the three men who left the expedition, they were not so lucky. They climbed out without any difficulty but on the third day away from the river they were killed by a band of unfriendly Indians.

Major Powell's second trip in 1871–72 included better equipment and enabled him to replace records that had been lost in upsets on the first expedition. Adding luster to his reputation as a national hero, Powell never went back to teaching geology. He spent several more years exploring and mapping the country north of the Colorado; then he went to Washington and for the rest of his life was head of the U.S. Geological Survey. He wrote several books about his canyon experiences but always commented about the first trip and never mentioned the second.

Frederick Dellenbaugh, who was seventeen years old when he joined Powell's second expedition, later wrote two books about his experiences. Sometimes, he said, when the river flowed smooth and calm, the men sang—some of them had pretty good voices. They sang old favorites and popular songs of the day such as "Come Where My Love Lies Dreaming," "What Are the Wild Waves Saying," "Annie Laurie," and "Seeing Nellie Home." Major Powell did a lot of singing himself, not that his voice was so good but because it helped him think and plan for the problems ahead. At other times, usually when they were floating smoothly along, the major or his second in command, Professor A. H. Thompson, would read aloud the poetry of Longfellow, Tennyson, Whittier, Robert Burns, or Sir Walter Scott.

But there were other times, Dellenbaugh wrote, when the Colorado became "a veritable dragon, loud in its dangerous lair, defiant, fierce, opposing utility everywhere, refusing absolutely to be bridled by Commerce, perpetuating a wilderness, prohibiting mankind's encroachments and in its immediate tide presenting a formidable host of snarling waters whose angry roar, reverberating wildly league after league between giant walls carved through the bowels of the earth, heralds the impossibility of human conquest and smothers hope."

Being the first into unexplored country gives the explorer a chance to name many of the new places. Powell did this in the Colorado canyons. Long before he reached the Grand Canyon he had named others: Flaming Gorge, Lodore, Desolation, Cataract, Labyrinth, and Marble. Other landmarks he named include Disaster Falls, Vasey's Paradise, Echo Rock, and Music Temple. He called one dangerous stretch of water Sockdolager Rapids, after the slang term meaning something outstanding, final, and hard to match.

One of the men called an especially muddy, alkaline, and undrinkable stream flowing into the Colorado a "Dirty Devil," and the name stuck. Later, to offset this, the major called another clear-water stream Bright Angel Creek. He also tried later to change the name of Dirty Devil to Fremont River, but the older name stuck. The Dirty Devil is formed in Utah by the joining of the Fremont and Muddy rivers, and it is augmented further by the flow from Poison Creek Canyon.

Major Powell was a scientist, and the accounts of his experiences are true even though some of them sound like tall stories. But his trips gave rise to some rather tall yarns. For example, in mid-August of 1869, Major Powell had not been heard from for many weeks and was given up for lost. It was then that a bearded, weary man boarded an eastbound Union Pacific train at Green River Station, Wyoming. He eased himself tiredly into a seat and, as the train rolled east, he let it be known that he was the sole survivor of Powell's lost expedition.

He told in great detail how he had watched from shore while Major Powell and the others were caught in a giant whirlpool and sucked down to death in the muddy Colorado. It happened, he said, near a dismal place called Brown's Hole. On the long, hard journey out, the lone survivor had lost everything but his life. Admiring fellow passengers promptly took up a collection, and the brave man was persuaded to accept it. Modestly, he pocketed the money. At the next stop he slipped off the train and disappeared.

By the time the train reached its destination in the East, news of Powell's successful trip through the canyon was making newspaper headlines. Meanwhile, a clever con artist had made the best of a good opportunity. Even the place of disaster was a tall tale, for Brown's Hole was actually a pleasant valley along the river.

Time and dams have brought changes to Powell's river and canyons: some 186 miles of the places Powell named and admired are now under water held behind Glen Canyon Dam. Included among these are Glen Canyon itself, Music Temple, and Labyrinth and Cataract canyons. Although the backed-up water that covers them is named Lake Powell, the major might not be happy with the results.

El Tovar, the finest in south rim hotel and eating accommodations, was opened by Fred Harvey and the Santa Fe Railroad in 1905.

CHAPTER II

TALES OF
TRAVEL AND TOURISM

To SAY THAT THERE WAS EVER A TIME WHEN MOST PEOPLE CHOSE NOT TO VISIT THE canyon, even though they passed within sixty miles of it, sounds like a tall story today. But before the mid-1880s, especially before there was a transcontinental railroad, the Grand Canyon was not a tourist attraction.

The California '49ers and, later, pioneers who traveled across country by wagon train or stagecoach were not interested in scenery. They saw plenty of scenery every day and on dusty roads they often inhaled it. Travelers in stagecoaches were bounced around too much to enjoy what they saw, while those in covered wagons traveled so slowly that any outstanding landmark might be visible for days at a time. Besides, the pioneers were looking for good farm land, valuable mineral deposits, or promising ranch sites; scenery was not on their list of desirables.

After the Union Pacific and Central Pacific railroads linked the nation in 1869, cross-country travel was much easier, faster, and more comfortable than travel by covered wagon or stagecoach. People gradually became interested in whatever unusual sights the country had to offer. A few pioneers drifted into a scenic area, saw possibilities in it, and began trying to sell their enthusiasm to others.

Two of the earliest pioneers for Grand Canyon tourism were "Captain" John Hance and William W. Bass, who arrived at the south rim in the early 1880s.

Both men liked what they saw and both began devising ways to share it with others, enabling them to make a living for themselves in the process.

Captain Hance operated out of Flagstaff but he had a homestead at Grand View Point on the south rim. He also staked mineral claims in the canyon and built a trail to them, a route still known as Hance's Trail. When tourists began visiting the area he offered his services as a guide. An advertisement he put in *The Arizona Champion* (Flagstaff) on 18 September 1886 made him one of the first travel agents in Arizona. It read:

> Being thoroughly conversant with all the trails leading to the Grand Canyon of the Colorado, I am prepared to conduct parties thereto at any time. I have a fine spring of water near my house on the rim of the Canyon, and can furnish accommodations for tourists and their animals.
>
> JOHN HANCE, Flagstaff, Arizona

As tourist literature, the ad was not very exciting but it did attract business.

The "accommodations" consisted of tents and a two-room "hotel" at Grand View Point where, Hance assured his prospective clientele, tourists would no longer have to brave the elements if a sudden storm arose. He also built a cabin at the bottom of the canyon to shelter the more adventurous visitors. Remains of Hance's cabin are still visited by rafters and backpackers. Hance even managed to get a U.S. postoffice named "Tourist" established at his headquarters on the rim and had himself appointed postmaster. More about Captain John Hance later.

William W. Bass also built more than fifty miles of trail into the canyon between 1885 and 1901, and at the bottom he had a small ferry to take tourists and their equipment across the Colorado River. Bass also operated a stage line from Williams, where people could leave the railroad for the ride to the canyon. Later, he moved his stage headquarters to Ash Fork in order to meet travelers coming up from Phoenix on the Santa Fe, Prescott & Phoenix Railroad. That line, which no longer carries passengers, was locally known as the "Pea-Vine."

While competition between Bass and Hance was not exactly cutthroat, each resorted to advertising when the need arose. Bass sang his own praises and announced his move from Williams to Ash Fork with the following ad, which appeared in the Prescott *Weekly Arizona Miner* on 15 April 1895.

> Cataract route, formerly Williams route. On May 1st and until further notice I will run regular stages between Ash Fork and the Grand Canyon of the Colorado River. Tourists are landed directly opposite Point Sublime at the head of Mystic Spring Trail reaching the Cliff Dwellings,

Grand Scenic Divide, Rains of Paradise, and Colorado River on horse-back. No rope ladders or toboggan slides by this route. Cataract Canyon, Supai Villages and Bridal Veil Falls reached by this route only. A commodious hotel, under the Harvey Eating House management, is now open at Ash Fork for the accommodation of this class of travel. Rates—$3.00 per day. The Santa Fe, Prescott & Phoenix makes liberal concessions to parties of 10 or more. For rates apply to F. A. Healy, G.P.A. (general passenger agent), Prescott or any agent of that line. I will run stages to suit the convenience of my patrons. Stage fare, round trip, $15. Parties of 10 or more, $12.50. Meals and beds, $.75 each. For further information please address W. W. Bass, prop., Ash Fork, A.T.

Hance and Bass were not the only ones interested in taking tourists to the Grand Canyon. Other stage lines were in operation on a more-or-less regular basis from as early as 1885. In the spring of 1892, the Santa Fe began regular (three times a week) stage service from Flagstaff to the canyon, covering a distance of sixty-five miles in twelve hours. The exact schedule, however, was subject to bad weather and breakdowns. From May through October, depending on how soon snow melted in the spring or fell in the fall, stages left Flagstaff at 7 a.m. on Mondays, Wednesdays, and Fridays and returned on Tuesdays, Thursdays, and Saturdays. There were three relay stations along the way where the four-horse teams were changed. A lunch stop at the second station—East Cedar Ranch, thirty-five miles from Flagstaff—cost passengers fifty cents a meal. The round trip fare was twenty dollars plus another dollar for supper and overnight lodging at Hance's "hotel."

A stage trip to the canyon was not the greatest, so far as comfort was concerned. The vehicles varied: there were mountain stages that looked like the traditional movie stagecoach, there were light passenger wagons, and even carriages. In chilly weather, closed buses were added. But the stages rocked on leather slings, and the wagons bounced on heavy metal springs. Even after the trails became fixed and worn, the metal-shod wheels bounced over rocks with bone-jarring frequency. In dry weather, the teams stirred up choking clouds of dust that the passengers "ate" for hours. In wet weather, there was mud, lots of it, splashed in every direction by sixteen iron-shod hooves. The pace was not, however, the hell-for-leather gallop that movie stagecoaches use.

As the stage lumbered through the pine-dotted countryside, the driver took an occasional pot-shot at a curious deer. At least once, so the report goes, the driver hit his deer and stopped long enough to clean out the carcass and load it on top of the luggage. "I need some meat at home," he explained to the passengers who watched in amazement. Passengers, too, could ride on top and practice their marksmanship as the stage rolled through jackrabbit country.

All things considered, the stage schedules were remarkably accurate. There were delays, of course. An experienced driver knew better than to turn his team loose at a stage stop. He kept one horse to ride while rounding up fresh horses and, because corrals were fairly large and the teams partly wild, this could take some time. In case of an accident, a wheel off, or other breakdown, passengers were expected to help the driver in every way possible.

In spite of discomforts, tourist travel to the Grand Canyon increased each year, and because it did, more comforts were added. From a total of sixty-seven visitors to the canyon in September of 1883, according to the Flagstaff *Coconino Sun,* a record number of nine hundred people visited the canyon in 1899, three hundred of them during July. Many of these early tourists recorded their impressions in Captain Hance's guest register. In 1892, for example, these were some of the thoughts recorded:

"July 9 [female visitor]: I have never witnessed anything like this. It scares me to even try to look down into it. My God, I am afraid the whole country will fall into this great hole in the ground."

"July 14 [male visitor]: By Joe! this canyon takes the whole shooting match."

"August 5 [male visitor]: The Grand Canyon is the most wonderful thing I have ever looked at. Surely worth seeing."

"August 25 [Texan and wife]: Went to the river and back; too tired to write more."

Stagecoach riders were not the only visitors to the canyon. Going there was becoming a sporting event, too. In 1896, the Coconino Cycling Club staged its third annual ride to the canyon with much fanfare in Flagstaff's daily *Coconino Sun.* More than fifty invitations were sent to bicycle enthusiasts near and far, and even abroad, but only thirteen hardy cyclists were on hand for the 6 a.m. start on 19 August: three of these were from Gallup, three from Albuquerque, one from Wingate, and the remaining six were from Flagstaff. They each paid ten dollars to participate, which included three nights at the canyon sleeping in tents, with meals provided.

They pedaled their bicycles over the stage route from Flagstaff, around the

San Francisco Peaks, past Sunset Crater, across a rolling prairie with the Painted Desert in view far off to the northeast, and up again into the forest along the rim. Rain in the afternoon made the last miles of the trail quite muddy, but the first three riders pedaled into view of the canyon at 6 p.m., two arrived at 9 p.m., and one came whistling down the hill to the hotel at 10 o'clock that night. Six riders gave up because of the mud and rode a stage from Moqui Station to the canyon. The thirteenth rider had bad luck: he broke the sprocket chain on his wheel and had to push his bike the rest of the way to the canyon.

After a good night of rest in the tents provided for them, the cyclists spent the next two days tramping down the trails, visiting the caves, and seeing the sights in general. They pedaled back to Flagstaff on 23 August, making the trip, mostly down grade, in eight hours. "The visitors who took part in the run were highly pleased with the trip," *The Coconino Sun* proudly reported, "and were loud in their praise of the Coconino Cycling Club for the courtesies extended to them."

People in the northern part of Arizona Territory had long hoped for a spur railroad to run north to the canyon from the main line through Flagstaff and Williams, serving ranches and mines along the way. In 1899, the Grand Canyon Railroad began building its roadbed and soon trains were running. But the mines were not as profitable as expected; in fact, many of them soon played out, business was not so good, and the company ran out of money. The line stopped at Coconino, eleven miles short of the canyon, and for two years stagecoaches met the trains there and carried passengers on to the rim.

In 1901, the Santa Fe bought the Grand Canyon line and completed the track, ending at the head of Bright Angel Trail, twelve miles west of Hance's hotel at Grand View Point. Passengers on the trains had an easy ride, but not so the engineer and fireman in the locomotives. The railroad right-of-way was not fenced, and often there would be ranch animals roaming on the track. There was no time to stop and scarcely time for the train crew to dodge a flying carcass as the engine zoomed along. Wild animals were no problem for they stayed off the tracks, but cattle, horses, burros, and sheep did not. Sheep were the worst, apparently, for their wool and tallow balled up under the wheels, fouled air lines to the brakes, and even caused derailments.

The Santa Fe arranged its schedule so that passengers from the East could get to the canyon with the least possible difficulty. One of their top trains, the California Limited, arrived at Williams from Chicago at 10:45 each night. Pullman cars routed to the canyon were switched from the main line to a siding, while cars returning from the canyon were switched to the Limited and taken on to the coast. The canyon train with its new consignment of cars left Williams at 5:30 a.m. and arrived at the canyon at 6:50 a.m. Passengers could sleep through it all and awake to a day of canyon sightseeing. They boarded the train again at 8:45 that evening and arrived at Williams at 10:00 p.m. There, the cars were switched to join the Limited and carried on west.

By 1902, horse-drawn stages were phased out, and the privately owned automobile was getting into the tourist picture. One of the most unusual of the vehicles was a Locomobile, which arrived in Flagstaff on 3 January 1902. Its proud owner bragged that it would make the run to the canyon in less than four hours. He was mistaken.

The Locomobile was a remarkable vehicle. It was steam powered and used either kerosene or gasoline for fuel. *The Coconino Sun* described it in detail:

> From bell to whistle it is a perfect locomotive. Its engines are 10-horse power high speed marine engines, copied after the United States torpedo boat type, fitted with water coil and flash boilers.
>
> There is a storage capacity for thirty gallons of oil and 57 gallons of water. The water reservoir is filled by a patent siphon operated by the engine's own steam. Its speed test, which was made between Toledo and Detroit, is 42 miles an hour under 175 pounds of steam. The tires of the machine are four inches in width, with solid rubber an inch and a half in thickness.
>
> The weight of this powerful machine, ready for the start, is about 2,200 pounds, and mud, snow, or ice cannot seriously impede its progress.

The people of Flagstaff were less enthusiastic than *The Coconino Sun* when they gathered to watch the Locomobile start its trip at 2:10 on Saturday afternoon, 4 January 1902. They gave it anywhere from six days to six years to make the journey. The vehicle started off in fine style and ran perfectly until it was out of town; then the troubles began.

First, there was trouble with the trailer, loaded with 110 gallons of water and fuel, photographic equipment, and baggage for the four passengers aboard the Locomobile. Because it was bearing down too heavily on the rear axle of the vehicle, the trailer had to be unloaded and repacked again. This done, the Locomobile ran on until dark. There was no moon, the kerosene lamps were dim, and finally the party stopped to avoid the risk of running into fallen trees or charred stumps along the way. Not expecting to be out after dark, the travelers had not packed any food or camping gear. Luckily, they were able to spend the night in a mountain cabin. Also bunking in the cabin were three cowboys who hospitably shared their supper of biscuits, honey, coffee, and freshly killed beefsteak with the hungry Locomobile crew.

They made a fresh start the next morning and ran along merrily for ten miles until the water gauge burst and they lost all their steam. A poor grade of gasoline complicated their problems, so they decided to abandon the trailer. Then a sprocket chain broke and they had to spend another night outdoors without supper or breakfast. By this time the Locomobile had used up all its cargo of water and fuel, so the four passengers left it on the trail and started toward the canyon on foot. One by one, three of them gave up. The fourth man finished the hike to the Grand View Hotel where he found supper, sympathy, and help for the others. The following day they telegraphed Flagstaff for gas, which arrived the day after. Five days after leaving Flagstaff they managed to get the Locomobile to the canyon. Then, after taking a lot of photographs and resting up for several days, the somewhat crestfallen owner drove his machine back to Flagstaff in about seven hours.

The day of automobile travel to the canyon had begun, and by 1912 a new Perry car made a record seventy-mile run from Flagstaff to the canyon in three hours and five minutes. This, *The Coconino Sun* proudly stated, is a great boost for "our good roads in northern Arizona." It also added that the same car had made the trip from Phoenix to Flagstaff without a single puncture, noting that the quality of tires was improving as well.

It would be years before the automobile would put the trains out of business. Pullman travel was in its heyday in the 1920s and continued to be popular through the 1950s. In the twenties and early thirties, it was not uncommon for the railroad to run two, three, or four sections of trains each day to the Grand Canyon. In 1920, the year after Grand Canyon became a national park, the Santa Fe carried 50,075 passengers to the canyon, compared with 10,260 people who arrived by automobile.

Central to the popularity of rail travel were the hotel and eating accommodations made available by Fred Harvey. Known as the proprietor of eating places along the railroads of the nation, Fred Harvey is still so well known, especially at Grand Canyon Village, that many people expect to meet him there in person. Yet today Fred Harvey is a corporation, not an individual; it is a subsidiary of AMFAC with headquarters in California. But first, meet Fred Harvey, the man.

His life was a success story, the poor-boy-makes-good kind that nineteenth-century America was proud of. Born in London in 1836, Fred Harvey came to the United States when he was fifteen years old. He got a job washing dishes in a New York restaurant for eight dollars a month. Six years later, at the age of twenty-one, he was operating a successful restaurant business in St. Louis. When the Civil War brought an end to that enterprise, he moved to Leavenworth, Kansas, and started over again as a ticket agent for the Chicago, Baltimore & Quincey Railroad. From this start, he worked up to general western freight agent, a job that called for a lot of traveling by rail.

Trains in those days did not carry diners; they scheduled twenty-minute stops at meal-times, and passengers had to grab a bite to eat in a hurry at eateries where the food was bad and the service was worse. Along with indigestion, the experience gave ex-restaurant owner Fred Harvey a great idea.

He presented his idea—that of providing food service to railroad travelers—to officials of the Atchison, Topeka & Santa Fe Railroad. The Santa Fe men were interested in anything that would lure passengers away from other lines, and if Fred Harvey's food and lodgings could do that, the railroad owners were willing to let him try. According to the agreement, the railroad would build and own the station hotels and restaurants, while Fred Harvey would manage them and provide good food and service at reasonable prices.

Harvey opened his first lunch room in 1886. His first effort was followed by a chain of restaurants, hotels, gift shops, and news stands stretching from Cleveland to Los Angeles and publicized as "3000 miles of hospitality." When he died of cancer in 1901, Fred Harvey left forty-five hotels and eating houses in operation along the Santa Fe route.

The food served in Fred Harvey restaurants was good, varied, and tasty. Refrigerated cars on the railroad made available the best grade of meat from Kansas City and the freshest fruits and vegetables from California. By his insistance on a "proper" atmosphere in his eating houses—men were expected to wear coats—Fred Harvey set such a standard of taste and decorum that he was often referred to as "the civilizer of the West."

To serve the meals, Fred Harvey hired polite, young ladies from the East, who were known as "Harvey girls." They were carefully trained as waitresses and dressed in prim black uniforms with white bib aprons. The girls were housed in dormitories under careful supervision; yet waiting on tables provided the perfect opportunity for meeting eligible men, and many Harvey girls married western pioneers and raised families on the frontier.

Following Fred Harvey's death, his eldest son, Ford, became president, his younger son, Byron, became vice president, and the Fred Harvey Company continued to grow as the Santa Fe extended its lines to more than twelve thousand miles and strove to attract more passengers and business in the West. The Santa Fe saw the attractions of the Grand Canyon as a part of this business and, with Fred Harvey (the company) as an able associate, advertising and building plans were begun on a railroad-owned hotel managed and operated by Fred Harvey.

In encouraging tourist travel, the Santa Fe and Fred Harvey were well aware of the Spanish background and history of the West. They already owned and operated hotels named for Spanish conquistadores: the Alvarado in Albuquerque, New Mexico, named for Captain Hernando de Alvarado; the Castenada in Las Vegas, New Mexico, named for Pedro de Castenada; and the Cardenas in Trinidad, Colorado, named for Don Garcia Lopez de Cardenas. As first projected, the hotel at Grand Canyon was to be called Bright Angel Tavern, but on second thought (and that in a hurry) the new establishment was named El Tovar, after Don Pedro de Tovar, the first Spaniard to "conquer" the Hopi province of Tusayan and learn about the Grand Canyon.

The new place was to be plush, and neither expense nor pain were spared in making it so. Designed by a Chicago architect, the one-hundred-room wooden structure was a combination of Swiss chalet and Norwegian villa. Logs to build it came from Oregon, and native Arizona boulders served as the stonework. It was furnished in a grand style, but also for comfort and easy relaxation. It had music and art rooms, a ladies' lounging room, a club room, plus roof gardens, a solarium, and a grotto. With construction completed in 1904, El Tovar cost a quarter of a million dollars, and when furnished, it was said to be "probably the most expensively constructed and appointed log house in America."

Fred Harvey people outdid themselves to make visitors comfortable. In the dining room, Harvey girls in their neat black dresses and white aprons served meals that were prepared by an Italian chef who had formerly worked in New York and Chicago clubs. The dining tables were bright with sparkling glasses, silverware, and fresh flowers. Shiny old brass dishes, antique Dutch and English platters, and native Indian ollas were displayed on plate rails along the walls. Tradition says that in the days before high-powered stains and wax polishes, the walls of the dining room were rubbed down every week with coffee to retain color, sheen, and neatness. To insure top quality food, the hotel had its own greenhouse for fresh vegetables, a herd of cows for milk, and chickens for eggs and poultry.

Water was always a problem at the canyon, as the first Spanish explorers discovered. To meet this need, the railroad hauled water every day in tank cars from Del Rio, 120 miles away. This continued until 1932 when a pumping station was built at Indian Gardens and water was piped up from there. (More recently, pipelines from Roaring Springs on the canyon bottom carry water to both rims.)

Rates at the El Tovar were four dollars a day and up, American plan. For guests on tighter budgets, the nearby Bright Angel Camp was operated European plan: rooms were one dollar a day, per person, and meals were served at the Harvey Cafe.

Fred Harvey made sure that his guests had every opportunity to see and enjoy the canyon's awesome beauty. Horse-drawn vehicles were available to take visitors to various scenic view points. The ten-mile trip to Dripping Springs cost four dollars each for three or more persons, or for less than three, there was an extra five dollar charge for a guide; for the trip to Hance's ranch and for using the trails to Moran and Bissell points, the charge was four dollars a day and five dollars for the guide, or $2.50 for half a day and the same for a guide. These were 1907 prices. Saddle horses were rented for four dollars per day, or $2.50 for half a day, with English, McClellan, Whitman, or Western stock saddles available. Ladies' divided skirts, gentlemen's overalls, hats, and other equipment for the trail could be rented at reasonable prices. All the visitor had to do was ask for what was needed at the hotel office.

The Santa Fe continued to encourage western tourist travel, stressing colorful Indian life, arts, and crafts in its advertisements. These ads shaped for all Americans the popular idea of what western Indians looked like. The Fred Harvey Company had extensive collections of Indian baskets, pottery, rugs, and jewelry, which were on display in the hotels and eating houses. Fred Harvey gift shops stocked Indian craft items that were for sale.

As the years passed, train travel became less and less popular, and by 1950 only 48,097 visitors arrived by train, compared with more than 500,000 who came by automobile. However, Fred Harvey (the company) has continued to be the chief concessionaire at the south rim despite the loss of its Santa Fe ally in 1969. Workers at the south rim number 1100 at the peak of the summer season and most of them are employed by Fred Harvey. Each employee is given a six-hour orientation, which includes a brief history of the Fred Harvey enterprises and a lesson in proper Grand Canyon lingo.

For example, in the old days visitors who arrived by train were called "dudes," and those coming by car were "sagebrushers." Now all visitors are referred to as "turkeys," while "savages" are the park's hired help. Further divisions among the help are: "pearl divers," who are dish washers; "heavers," who are waitresses; "pillow punchers," who are tent girls and chambermaids; and "bubble queens," who are laundry girls. Drivers and chauffuers are "gear jammers" or just plain "jammers," while the porters and bell boys are "pack rats" or just "rats." Permanent employees of the Fred Harvey Company are called "lifers," and rangers assigned to law enforcement or to search and rescue teams are known as "danger rangers."

The railroad days are over, but not forgotten; Fred Harvey accommodations keep the memory alive. His name is still mentioned so often, and always in the present tense, that newcomers expect to meet the man somewhere on the premises. And on rare occasions, some tourist turns up at the main office and requests an interview with Mr. Fred Harvey. Few can forget the great alliance that was forged between Harvey and the railroad in bringing tourist accommodations to the Grand Canyon.

John Hance (second rider) and Teddy Roosevelt on the Bright Angel Trail.

CHAPTER III

CAPTAIN HANCE,
CHAMPION YARN SPINNER

THE WAY CAPTAIN JOHN HANCE TOLD IT TO EASTERN VISITORS, HE FIRST ARRIVED at the Grand Canyon along with a buffalo herd that was migrating north from Texas. Somewhere in the Lone Star state, Hance had climbed a tree, and when the herd went by he dropped onto the back of a big buffalo bull. He rode that bull for two weeks, until the herd reached Arizona. If anyone asked, and someone usually did, what Hance had to eat during all that time, the captain had a ready answer. "Oh," he would say, "with that hump of buffalo right in front of me I had plenty of meat. You know, buffalo hump is the tastiest part of the animal."

Captain Hance spent the last dozen or so years of his life telling tales to tourists. He became a fixture at the canyon, famous as a teller of tall tales. He told them so well that many a visitor left the canyon more than half convinced that most of the stories Hance told really had happened.

Not much is known about Hance's early years. He was born during the late 1830s at Cowans Ferry, Tennessee. Like many of his time and age, he fought in the Civil War, but his title of captain was an honorary one acquired informally and much later. He claimed to have fought on both sides, first for the Confederacy and later, after being captured, for the Union. When the war ended, he was mustered out at Fort Leavenworth, Kansas. There, he and his brother George got jobs with a mule train owned by "Tame" Bill Hickok, brother of the more famous "Wild" Bill Hickok. The mule train took them to Camp Verde in Arizona

31

Territory, where George Hance settled, served as justice of the peace for forty-five years, and became a leading citizen of Yavapai County.

"My brother George is a fine man," Captain Hance observed, "but he has a habit of talking to himself. One time I asked him, 'Brother George, why do you talk to yourself?' 'I've got two good reasons,' George answered. 'I like to hear a smart man talk, and I always like to talk to a smart man.' "

Leaving his brother in Camp Verde, John Hance moved on to Williams. He probably saw the canyon first during a prospecting trip in 1883. He liked what he saw so well that he remained in the vicinity for the rest of his life.

As the years passed, competition for the tourist trade grew stiffer. Hance sold his trails in 1895 and bought a house in Flagstaff in 1898, but by 1901 he was back in the canyon managing some asbestos mines and guiding more tourists. Meanwhile, the railroad had arrived and with it came Fred Harvey and El Tovar.

Captain Hance's reputation as a teller of tales had grown over the years, and Fred Harvey recognized an asset when he saw one. Hance was retained, more or less informally, as resident "character" and tourist attraction, with room and board provided by Fred Harvey. The old man dressed the part; that is, he continued to look like the old-time prospector he had been. This was real "local color" and the tourists loved it.

Captain Hance knew a good thing, too. He had a place to stay, eats provided, an admiring audience for his tales, and best of all, he was close to his beloved canyon. What more could an old man want? Hance was happy, but he knew better than to rest on his laurels. His mind was constantly busy thinking of new tales to tell the tourists. He shared this concern with friends. "If I can make the tourists believe that a frog eats boiled eggs," he once told a woman who had known him for years, "I'll do it. And then I'll make them believe that he carries the eggs a mile to find a rock to crack them on."

Hance's most famous story was his fog yarn and he told it many times with slight variations. Nearly all visitors to the canyon, who later wrote accounts of their trip, mentioned the story. To tell it best, Hance would wait for a foggy day when the canyon depths were shrouded in mist. Then, with a pair of snowshoes slung over his shoulder, he would amble up to a group of tourists seated on the porch at El Tovar.

"Fog's about right to cross," he would say, unslinging the snowshoes and preparing to lash them on. Then he would walk over to the canyon edge, stick a foot out into space, and pretend to test the fog. "Yep," he would say. "It's just right for crossing. But it's shorter to the north rim if I start from Yaki Point. Watch tonight and you'll see my campfire over there." With that, Captain Hance shouldered his snowshoes and marched off to disappear among the trees in the direction of Yaki Point. He would be seen no more that day.

The next afternoon he would reappear. "Did you see my fire on the north rim last night?" he would inquire. If the answer was yes, he would nod approvingly. If the answer was no, he would shrug and say, "Well, I couldn't see your lights over here, either." Then he would continue. "The fog was pretty thick going over and I made good time. But coming back was different. The fog was thin and it sagged under me at every step. It was like walking on a feather bed and I now feel plumb wore out. Guess I'll go take a nap before supper. If any of you folks want to try it," he would ask over his shoulder as he walked off, "I'll be glad to lend you my snowshoes next time she fogs up good and solid."

On some occasions, he would tell of the time when the fog cleared suddenly and he was marooned on a peak in the canyon for several days without food or water. When the fog did return, it was not so thick as before, but by that time Hance had lost so much weight that he was able to get back anyway. Even so, he almost hit bottom while crossing some spots where the fog was especially thin. "I sure filled up on food when I got back," was the way he would end that story.

A favorite breakfast-table yarn went back to the time he was a prospector in the canyon. He planned to spend the winter in Flagstaff and he judged the time of year by the end of his grub and the onset of the first snowfall. When it came time to leave the canyon, he started out on snowshoes but fell and hurt his ankle so that he had to return to his cabin. There was nothing left to eat but half a jar of sorghum molasses and a box of Babbitt's Best Soap. So Hance prepared a mixture of soap and molasses in his frying pan, slicing the soap into flakes and adding a few shavings from an old boot leg to make the mixture as tasty as possible.

"Ladies and gentlemen, that was all I had to eat for a week," the captain would conclude while pouring syrup on a third helping of pancakes. "I tell you frankly, and I expect you to believe me, I have never liked the taste of soap from that day to this." Then he would shovel in a mouthful of breakfast while the others at the table stared at him in dead silence. No one knew whether to laugh or not.

Knowing that eastern visitors liked to hear thrilling tales about narrow escapes from Indians, Hance had a number of these, like the following, for example.

While leading a group of tourists along a rim trail, he would point to a series of blazes all the same height on tree trunks beside the way. "See those blazes?" he would say. "Do you know how they got there?" When nobody did, he would explain. "I scraped them there myself with my knees and elbows. I did it one day when my horse, Roaney, and me were running away from a bunch of Apaches on the war path."

Or, pointing to a tall ponderosa pine, he would say, "See that tree over there? It saved my life one time. An Indian was out hunting and he stirred up a bear. The bear got away from the Indian but he was real angry. Then I came along and the bear chased me. I ran for that tree in a hurry." "But, Captain Hance," a tourist was supposed to object, "the lowest limb on that pine tree is thirty feet up. How in the world did you manage to reach it?" "Oh, I took a running jump," the captain would answer. "I sure missed it on the way up, but I caught it coming down."

Then there was the time when a band of Indians chased Roaney and him into a narrow side canyon. The canyon got narrower and narrower until finally Hance and his horse were stuck fast. "Then what happened?" the tourists would ask. "Oh, those Indians killed me," the captain would reply.

Old Roaney was a fine horse and the captain was proud of him. "He was a great jumper," the old man would reminisce. "One time I bet a friend of mine that Old Roaney could jump the canyon if he took a long enough run for it." "Could he do it?" the admiring audience would inquire. "He did his durndest," Hance would continue. "I took him back a mile or so to give him a good long run. By the time we reached the canyon rim he was going full gallop. He made a good take-off but the start was too short. Halfway across I saw he wasn't going to make it." "Then what did you do?" the audience would gasp. "Oh, I just turned him around and we went back to the rim again."

Hance did not have a wife and he had an explanation for that, too, in case anyone asked. "I did get married once," he would say, "and I brought my bride here to the canyon. But one day she slipped off the edge of the trail and broke her leg in the fall." "How terrible!" someone would exclaim. "Yes," the captain would agree. "Poor gal, with that broken leg, I had to shoot her."

Sometimes the tale was different. When she fell, the bride broke both legs and it took Hance two days to reach her. After she recovered, she had had enough of the canyon so she went back East and got a divorce. That was the end of the romance.

In another of his adventure tales, Hance was once caught in a side canyon by a Colorado River flood. There was no way to escape, so he had to wait until the water went down. Before the flood ended, his food supply was exhausted. "How did you survive without starving?" his listeners would ask. "Well, you see, I had a plug of chewing tobacco in my pocket," Hance would explain, "so I cut it up into little pieces and threw some of them into the water. Then I got me a mesquite branch from a pile of driftwood and waited. 'Twasn't long before I was using that branch to hit the fish over the head when they came up to spit. I was getting pretty tired of eating raw fish by the time the flood was over."

The Colorado River and its floods supplied plenty of material for his stories. One day, while standing with a group of tourists on the rim, a lady asked him, "Captain Hance, I don't see any water in the canyon. Is this the dry season or does it never have any water in it?" Gazing at her earnestly with his faded blue eyes, the old man answered, "Madam, in the early days, many's the time I have rode my horse up here and let him drink right from this very place where we now stand."

As for mud in the Colorado, he would tell of the time when the mud was so thick that, even though the water tasted wet, he needed something to dig it up with. Lacking a shovel, he lay down on the bank to take a drink, but the water was so thick that it stuck in his throat and threatened to choke him. "I tried to bite it off," he recalled, "but my teeth were too poor for that. Finally, I managed to pull my hunting knife out of my boot and cut off the water."

At Moran Point there was a split in the rocks that Hance called Fat Woman's Misery. That was because one day he was leading a party of easterners along the rim at that point. They all squeezed through the narrow opening except one fat woman who got stuck. "I pushed and pulled," Hance said, "but she was stuck fast. There were only two things that could be done and I gave her the choice. She could stay there and starve, or I could blow her out with dynamite. She chose the dynamite so I went and got a couple of sticks and lighted the fuse. There was a big bang and a lot of rocks flying around but, when the dust settled, there she was free and sitting on a rock. 'Madam, how do you feel?' I asked her. 'Why, Sir,' she answered just a little dazed, 'I feel first rate, but the jolt gave me a little toothache.' "

His opinion of tourists was not always the highest. "The canyon's not what it used to be," he would complain. "It's not as deep as it was, either. The damn tourists kick so much gravel into it that they're filling it up."

Another loss to the tourists, according to Hance, was the tip of the index finger on his right hand. "I wore it plum off," he would explain, "pointing out the scenery to eastern visitors."

Whenever a party of tourists prepared to go down the Bright Angel Trail, Captain Hance had some words of warning. "You must understand," he told them, "that when you get down to the bottom of the canyon and reach the bank of the Colorado River you will find the weather very warm. Some days you can't imagine how hot it is. Why, I give you my word, I have been down there when it was so hot it melted the wings off the flies." "But, Captain," an incredulous lady from New England is supposed to have objected, "how do the tourists stand it?" "Madam," the captain answered solemnly, "I have never yet seen a tourist with wings."

Presence or absence of snakes in the canyon depended on Hance's mood and on the timidity of his audience. To discourage a tourist from wandering too far from camp, Hance claimed that the canyon was full of snakes—thousands of them at every turn of the trail. They formed daisy chains to get across chasms or down steep cliffs. They even hunted in packs, like wolves. After such descriptions, nobody ventured far from the safety of camp.

On the other hand, to reassure a timid lady, Hance would declare that there were no snakes at all in the canyon. There had been, he would add; in fact, one morning he had watched four hundred of them at Indian Gardens, all crawling in a circle. The hours passed and the circle grew smaller and smaller as each snake swallowed the tail of the one in front. "By evening," he would conclude, "there was not a snake left because they had all swallowed each other. To this day, I have not seen another snake in the canyon."

Another female visitor, who was interested in botany, had him help her collect leaves. "You know, Captain Hance," she said, "a tree is a wonderful organism. It really breathes." Hance looked at her and nodded solemnly. "I'm pleased to hear you say that, Ma'am," he said. "It explains something that has puzzled me for a long time. I used to camp under a big mesquite tree, and night after night it kept me awake with its snoring."

As for the fish in the Colorado, there were big ones, but not as big as they used to be. During his prospecting days, Hance was fixing breakfast in Red Canyon at Sockdolager Rapid when he saw a fish start up river. At noon he looked again and saw the middle of the fish going by. It was sunset by the time he saw the tail go by. "One day I caught a fish almost as big as that and tied it to a tree with a $5/16$-inch rope. I ate on him for six weeks," the old man concluded.

Children who visited the canyon all loved Captain Hance and his stories. The captain, for his part, never tired of telling his youthful audiences how he, personally, had dug the great gorge. There were several versions of this story. In one version he would point to the San Francisco Peaks and explain. "See those mountains? I piled them up with the dirt I dug out of the canyon."

There is another version of this story that was told about Hance rather than by him. It came to light after his death. In this one Hance simply claimed to have dug the canyon, and he told the story until one day a four-year-old listener asked: "But Captain Hance, if you dug that big hole, what did you do with the dirt?" For once, the captain was at a loss for an answer. So he never told that story again, but the child's question bothered him for the rest of his life. When he was on his death bed, some of his last words to his friends were, "Where do you suppose I could have put that dirt?"

The years passed, and Captain Hance did grow old. Winters at the canyon were too severe for him so during those months he lived at the Weatherford Hotel in Flagstaff. Late in 1918, the old man caught a chill that turned into pneumonia. The hotel was no place for a sick man, and Captain Hance needed constant care. The place he could get it was at the Coconino County Hospital for the Indigent— better known as the "poor farm." It was set up to care for people too poor or too old to care for themselves. Local doctors took turns coming out from town to visit patients for there was no doctor in residence.

Although he was not a charity patient, John Hance's name is listed on page twenty-seven of the hospital's ledger as one of the Coconino County Indigent, admitted to the hospital on 9 December 1918. He died there a few weeks later.

He is buried in the cemetery at the south rim, just west of the visitors' center and close to the Shrine of the Ages. His last resting place is not within sight of the canyon, as he wished it to be, but it is within easy walking distance. The bronze tablet on his headstone reads:

Captain John Hance
First locator on Grand Canyon
Arizona pioneer, trail builder and guide.
Died Jany. 6th, 1919 Aged 80 years

The grave is marked at his head and feet by two tall native boulders. As befits the teller of tall tales, these boulders, by actual measurement, are twelve and one-half feet apart.

Kolb Brothers Studio and home at the head of Bright Angel Trail.

CHAPTER IV

PHOTOGRAPHER'S TALES

THE GRAND CANYON IS A PHOTOGRAPHER'S PARADISE. IF ALL THE PICTURES EVER taken there were stacked together, they would fill the main gorge and several side canyons. Few people visit the area without some sort of camera, and so equiped, no one leaves without taking a few pictures, whether they be simple snapshots or carefully planned art studies.

Today a casual canyon visitor uses an Instamatic® camera, while the real photography buff has at least one good camera, probably a 35mm, plus a wide angle lens, a telephoto and/or zoom lens, some special filters, and a tripod. No matter how much equipment a modern photographer chooses to carry, his load is light when compared with the equipment used by those who first photographed the canyon scenery.

Major Powell had to depend on word pictures to describe what he saw on his first trip through the canyon. On his second trip, however, a photographer was on hand. Also, at the same time Powell was traveling down the Colorado, another government-sponsored survey party led by army Lieutenant George M. Wheeler was traveling up the river and into the canyon from the west. That party also included a photographer, and one can only speculate which man took the first picture within the limits of the Grand Canyon. Lieutenant Wheeler's photographer was a young Irishman named Timothy O'Sullivan. Major Powell had several cameramen; the first was a rather grumpy chap named E. O. Beaman, who stayed with the expedition only six months and then went off to photograph the country on his own.

Photography was a complicated affair in the 1870s, and photographers had many problems to contend with. Cameras were big, clumsy boxes. Roll or sheet film had not been perfected and exposures were made on glass plates by what was called a "wet plate" process; that is, a glass plate was coated with a sticky mixture called collodian, sensitized in a silver nitrate bath, and exposed in the camera. Then, while still wet, the picture on the plate had to be developed in another bath and fixed in still another.

To take pictures in the canyon, the photographer had to carry along his camera, glass plates, chemicals, and bath trays, as well as a darkroom tent to work in. He had to take all this wherever he went to make pictures—up cliffs, down canyons, across rocky beaches. He could not work without them. Wet plates required an exposure of thirty to sixty seconds with an f/16 lens in bright sunlight, a speed much too slow to stop the rush of the river. For that reason, the early shots show smooth stretches of water instead of rapids, and the Colorado looks tame and gentle with a surface as smooth as a lake. Beaman tried to take pictures of Powell's boats going through the rapids, but his wet plates were too slow and the attempt was unsuccessful. Book illustrations that show Powell's boats in violent rapids are always drawings, not photographs.

Modern photographers can stop a rapid in full fury with shutter speeds up to 1/1000th of a second or even faster. Early photographers had to focus on motionless canyon scenery for their effects, and their pictures were black and white or toned with gold to a pleasing red-brown color. Modern photographers can record the river's violent action in color with both still and motion picture cameras.

Photographer O'Sullivan took nearly three hundred pictures in the canyon using glass plates and developing them on the spot. So far, so good, but in the long shipment back to Washington, D.C., most of the plates were damaged or broken, and less than a dozen of his canyon pictures survived.

Beaman had better luck with his photographs, but he had to contend with the major's nephew, Clement C. Powell, as an assistant. Clem Powell was a pleasant fellow but he never mastered photography. He was the kind of cameraman who, today, takes a picture with his thumb over the lens, forgets to take off the lens cap, or opens the camera with the film still exposed inside it. Whether it was Clem's inept help, or some other reason that caused Beaman to leave the Powell expedition, the major had only Clem to depend on for a time. Clem's diary shows what troubles he had, troubles he was inclined to blame on the departed Beaman.

For example, on 4 January 1872, Clem wrote, "Fixed my things this morning and got ready for taking pictures, but the chemicals would not work and the instruments were not worth a cent and my whole outfit is nothing but Beaman's cast off things."

Days passed and Clem's woes continued, as his diary indicates.

Jan. 12: Tried picture taking; did not succeed very well.

Jan. 18: After breakfast was over I put up my dark tent and went to work, but 'twas no go. Finally concluded it was the water. Fixed and refixed my chemicals, filtered them, sunned my bath, etc., etc. By that time 'twas dark.

Jan. 19: After breakfast once more tried my chemicals and though I worked hard all day took only 4, and they nothing extra. There is something the matter I can't explain. I think it is the water.

Entries on 22, 23, and 25 January told the same sad tale of failure. On 26 January, Clem wrote: "Spent a miserable night. Was thinking or dreaming of pictures all night long; was glad when day at last appeared."

On 5 February, Frederick Dellenbaugh noted Clem's return from a picture-taking trip in Kanab Canyon. Clem had "met with bad luck and did not get a single negative. The silver bath got out of order, and the horse bearing the camera fell off a cliff and landed on top of the camera, which had been tied on the outside of the pack, with a result that need not be described."

Another member of Powell's party, Jack Hillers, was appointed as Clem's assistant. Originally hired as a boatman, "Jolly Jack" mastered the camera and took very good pictures. His diary also records poor Clem's photographic problems. On 20 February 1872, Hillers wrote: "This morning I was installed as assistant photographer. Clem tried to take some pictures but failed, bath being out of order—fixed it—while manipulating he upset it—so much for the first day."

Hillers continues on 22 February: "Put up the dark tent—Clem put the bath in it open, started to a spring for some water about a quarter of a mile from camp. On our return, lo, our tent had blown over and the bath spilled again. Tried another which he upset a third time." Clearly, Clem Powell was no photographer.

Jack Hillers, however, continued as the expedition's cameraman. Many of the photographs used to illustrate Major Powell's later writings bear the name of J. K. Hillers, photographer.

The next major camera project got under way in 1889–90 when the Brown-

Stanton survey party set out to plot a railroad route along the Colorado and through the Grand Canyon. The line was to be the Denver, Colorado & Pacific Railroad. Frank M. Brown was president of the railroad company and leader of the expedition. Robert B. Stanton was chief engineer.

Franklin A. Nims, the photographer, was to take pictures all along the way to show that the route was possible. He was better equipped for picture taking than his predecessors; by 1889, transparent film had been invented, and Nims did not have to carry bulky chemicals and fragile glass plates to work with.

The railroad surveyors, however, were not equipped for the hazardous river journey. President Brown forgot to order life preservers; he and two other men drowned, and the survivors gave up temporarily. Engineer Stanton reorganized the project, and a better equipped crew returned to the river.

This time it was photographer Nims who had bad luck. On the river, water soaked some of his supplies, sand got into his equipment, and the wind blew his camera over a cliff, but each time he managed to dry, clean, or repair the damaged equipment. Then real disaster struck. While climbing a rock wall to take a picture on New Year's Day 1890, Nims missed his footing and fell twenty-two feet; he struck his head, broke his ankle, and remained unconscious for eleven days. His companions carried him out of the canyon, hauling him up 1700 feet in a two-and-one-half-mile climb that took eight hours. On the top, he was placed in a wagon and taken to Lee's Ferry, thirty miles away. It was there that he regained consciousness on 12 January.

"I must have a doctor at once," he said. But the nearest doctor was at Kanab, Utah, ninety miles away and he could not be sent for until spring. Two days later a Mormon family came by in a wagon on their way to New Mexico. "I want them to take me to the railroad," Nims said. He was still flat on his back and partially paralyzed. The Mormons agreed, and for eighty-five dollars they took Nims to Winslow, Arizona, 185 miles away.

The trip took eleven days, and when they arrived, there was no room in the hotel. Nims managed to find lodging in a house, and the next day the Santa Fe Railroad doctor began the process of setting the photographer's bones and reducing his dislocations. Fifteen days later, Nims was carried to a Pullman and taken to Denver for more treatment. The Union Pacific surgeon there found and set another broken bone—five weeks between breaking and setting—but announced that the other breaks were mending. Seven weeks after his accident, on 20 February, Nims was able to eat solid food again. On 15 June, he wore a shoe for the first time and discarded his crutches but he used a cane for another month. Later he published two accounts of the expeditions, but only his diaries—he kept two of them—mention the accident and his injuries.

Nims was about thirty years old at the time of his accident and he lived to know his grandchildren. Photographers were strong in those days—they had to be.

Last of the canyon pioneer cameramen were Ellsworth and Emery Kolb, brothers from Pennsylvania. Ellsworth, the elder, arrived at the south rim in 1901, and Emery arrived a year later. Emery was interested in photography and he found a small photo gallery in Williams that was for sale. Somehow, the brothers managed the $425 needed to buy it and, before another year passed, they were established close to the head of the Bright Angel Trail, where they could take pictures of tourists starting down into the canyon. By the time the tourists returned, their pictures were developed, printed, and ready for sale.

Like other canyon pioneers, the Kolbs had a water shortage problem, and until 1928, water good enough to use in developing pictures had to be brought from a source eleven miles away. In emergencies, or for faster work, Emery would run the four and one-half miles from the rim to Indian Gardens, develop the film in the spring water there, and run back to the rim again. Sometimes he made the nine-mile round trip twice in one day.

Besides buying their own on-the-trail portraits, tourists also wanted to buy pictures of the canyon, and the Kolbs were willing to oblige. Their search for scenery carried them into many areas that were little known or never before explored. These excursions gave rise to another ambition: still pictures were fine, but what the Kolbs wanted to do was make a motion picture record of a boat trip through the canyon. In 1911, they decided to do it.

On 8 September 1911, they set out from Green River, Wyoming, in two specially built boats and hoped to reach the foot of Bright Angel Trail in about six weeks. In addition to the usual camping and river-running equipment, they also carried three film cameras, two plate cameras—one 8" x 10" and one 5" x 7"—and a hand-cranked movie camera of the type used in Hollywood. They also carried a plentiful supply of plates and films, a large cloth darkroom, and whatever chemicals they might need to test the picture results along the way. They had very little experience in making movies and they were not sure the cameras could take the rough treatment they were about to get. Nevertheless, as Ellsworth later wrote, "It was our secret hope that we could bring out a record of the Colorado as it is, a living thing, armed as it were with teeth, ready to crush and devour."

By the time the Kolbs made their trip through the canyon, the Colorado held few mysteries. Enough people had braved its dangers and survived, so that the obstacles were at least known if not completely understood. Even so, for two men in two boats to make the trip was quite a feat. Most other exploring parties had more manpower than that to run the rapids, portage around dangerous water, or get the boats through by lining them from shore. There were upsets, narrow escapes, and instances when the movie camera got thoroughly wet and the exposed film was ruined. But the brothers persisted and their accumulation of good pictures grew.

To begin with, the cameraman took action shots from shore while the boatman piloted his craft through a rapid; they also took shore pictures from the boats as they rowed along in quiet water. But they wanted more action; they wanted to show what it was really like to ride through a rapid. To do this, they tied their two boats together, stern to stern. Ellsworth, in the front, forward-facing boat, used the oars and steered, while Emery, the camera operator, sat in the bow of the second boat, as far back as he could get, with the motion picture camera in front of him. He held the camera down with his chin, braced both legs against the sides of the boat, held on with his left hand, and turned the crank of the movie camera with his right.

With this arrangement, they managed through two small rapids. The trailing boat, with no oarsman to control it, bucked like a bronco and almost tossed the cameraman out, but Emery hung on and cranked away, getting some usable pictures. After that attempt, however, they decided not to tackle a larger rapid. Once was enough; they had captured all the action they cared to and they did not wish to trust their luck any further.

As they had planned, the Kolbs traveled the Colorado canyons—Flaming Gorge, Lodore, Whirlpool, Split Mountain, Desolation, Cataract, Glen, Marble, and Grand—and arrived at the foot of Bright Angel Trail on 16 November 1911. On 19 December, they continued their trip and arrived at Needles on 18 January 1912. Then in May of 1913, Ellsworth finished the final four hundred miles from Needles to the Gulf of California. He later wrote a book entitled *Through the Grand Canyon from Wyoming to Mexico* describing the entire project.

Meanwhile, Emery took the motion-picture film and went on an extensive lecture tour; at that time illustrated lectures were considered the height of entertainment. When the tour was over, the Kolbs continued to show portions of the film and give the lecture in their studio on the edge of the canyon. It ran continuously from 1915 until Emery's death in 1976—a longer run than any other motion picture of its time.

The brothers continued their close association with canyon photography, with time out for service in the Signal Corps and for work with the National Geographic Society and the United States Geological Survey. Ellsworth moved to California in 1924, but Emery continued to live and work on the canyon rim, having occasional problems with the National Park Service and sometimes with the Fred Harvey people. He made his last river trip in 1974, and by that time the Colorado had been tamed by Glen Canyon Dam. Control of the river flow and use of big rubber rafts made running the rapids a picnic, he said, and added, "No one will ever know the Colorado as it really was. It's too late."

No modern photographer will know the problems met and solved by the early canyon cameramen, with their heavy cameras, their fragile wet plates, their chemicals, and their dark tents. Those days are gone, and no photographer in his right mind will regret their passing.

Phantom Ranch along Bright Angel Creek at the bottom of Grand Canyon. The guest ranch was designed by architect Mary Jane Colter and built by Fred Harvey in 1922.

CHAPTER V

PHANTOM RANCH
AND THE
WOMAN WHO DESIGNED IT

WOMEN HAVE PLAYED MUCH DIFFERENT ROLES IN CANYON HISTORY THAN THEIR male counterparts. The Spanish explorers were all male, as were the mountain men, prospectors, trappers, explorers, and surveyors. It was rough, rugged country; there was nothing gentle or feminine about it.

Of course, women were along on some expeditions: Indian women, who did the cooking, the camp chores, and looked after the welfare and comfort of the male explorers, were often present. Then there were the "respectable" wives, who waited at home, worried about their long-absent men, took care of the children (if any), and in general kept the home fires burning while their husbands, sons, brothers, or other male relatives were braving the Colorado or exploring the canyon country. Boats may have been named for wives or sweethearts, but the ladies themselves were usually absent from the expeditions.

Take, for example, the Powell expeditions. Both expeditions were all male, but when preparations were under way for the second one in the spring of 1871, Mrs. Powell did accompany her husband west, as did Mrs. Thompson, the major's sister and wife of Prof. A. H. Thompson, Powell's second in command. But the women had to wait in Salt Lake City while their men rode the river and explored.

Emma Dean Powell gave birth to a daughter that summer. When the child was three months old, she and Mrs. Powell joined the major at his winter camp near Kanab, where they lived in a tent, and a big clothes basket served as the baby's cradle. In February, the major took his wife and daughter back to Salt Lake City, then went on to Washington to ask congress for funds to continue his exploration and mapping of the river country.

Mrs. Thompson also joined her husband in camp and stayed on when the Powells departed. Ellen Powell Thompson had her brother's courage and daring; she would have made a good explorer. When she was taken for a short ride upstream to see what the canyon was like from a boat, she was enthusiastic. Later, when her husband took her on a brief run through two small rapids, she declared that she "enjoyed the exhilaration of descending the swift rushing water." Nonetheless, she had to wait on shore, living in a tent pitched in a Mormon leader's garden in Kanab, while the expedition continued its river run. Her dog, Fuzz, and one of the Mormon women were her closest companions. Ladies of her generation and social station were not included in exploring expeditions.

In the early 1880s, another breed of woman began to emerge who was every bit as daring and curious as her male predecessors. Mrs. Edward E. Ayer, wife of a Flagstaff sawmill owner, gained the distinction of being the first white woman to accompany her husband and family down to the river and back via the Hance Trail. More tourists followed, and in 1892 one of these was Miss Ada Diefendorf, a music teacher from Worcester, New York, who made the horseback trip to Havasu Canyon with William W. Bass as guide. Two years later, she and Bass were married. They lived at the Bass Camp, where Ada became the first white woman to raise a family on the south rim of the canyon.

It was Mary Elizabeth Jane Colter, architect, designer, and artist, who finally gave a woman's touch to canyon development. Many of the buildings she designed—Hopi House, Hermit's Rest, Bright Angel Lodge, the Lookout Tower, and Phantom Ranch—are still intact today. It was her artistic taste that gave a natural, southwestern flavor to Fred Harvey's establishments. She was one woman executive in an otherwise all-male company, and she held her own in it for more than forty years.

Mary Colter was an unusual woman in many ways. Born in Pittsburgh, Pennsylvania, in 1869 of Irish immigrant parents, she grew up in St. Paul, Minnesota, where, fortunately for her, the public schools stressed art and music. She chose art as a career, graduated from the California School of Design in San Francisco, and also studied architecture with a practicing architect. In a day when architects were few in number, and women architects were fewer still, Mary Colter dreamed of designing and decorating buildings.

Her first jobs, however, were teaching art and mechanical drawing in high school, which she did for fifteen years. Meanwhile, in the summer of 1902, she got her first part-time job with the Fred Harvey Company. The company was expanding and needed "a decorator who knew Indian things and had imagination" to arrange the Indian building that adjoined the new Alvarado Hotel in Albuquerque, New Mexico. Colter was hired and did the job well. Her second job for Fred Harvey was to design Hopi House next to El Tovar on the south rim. Opened on 1 January 1905, Hopi House is still a place to see and buy Indian arts and crafts at the canyon.

Not until 1910 did Mary Colter get a permanent, full-time job with Fred Harvey. From then until she retired—in 1948 at the age of 79—she was busy designing, decorating, and/or redecorating Fred Harvey hotels, restaurants, and railway station facilities. It was the ideas and handwork of Mary Colter that gave most Americans (and Europeans) their lasting impressions of Indians and the Southwest.

Phantom Ranch, at the bottom of the canyon on the bank of Bright Angel Creek, was the result of increasing tourist business after World War I, especially after the suspension bridge was built across the Colorado River. When visitors no longer had to cross the river on a scary cable car, more of them made the trip and, once across the river, they needed a place to stay.

The pleasant area at the mouth of Bright Angel Creek was the ideal place. Anasazi Indians had homes and farms there long before the Spaniards, and later Powell had camped there on his first trip through the canyon. Coming down from the north rim in the early 1900s, David Rust built a camp there and later played host to Teddy Roosevelt and his hunting party in 1913.

In 1921, Fred Harvey and the Santa Fe obtained permission from the National Park Service to build on the site of Rust's Camp, and Mary Colter was appointed designer for the buildings. She used native stone and a plan that made the one-story cabins blend in with the natural surroundings. She also named the place Phantom Ranch after Phantom Creek, a small stream that joins Bright Angel Creek a short distance above the ranch. Cartographers had earlier named the creek because of the misty, phantom-like haze in the side canyon from which it came. The name is intriguing, and anyone with imagination can dream up a number of ghost stories to go with it.

When Phantom Ranch opened for guests in the spring of 1922, designer Mary Colter and her sister Harriet were present for the celebration. Both made the trip by mule; Mary Jane probably enjoyed the trip, although her sister, who was a semi-invalid, probably did not.

In its early years, Phantom Ranch was a small and exclusive resort. As the "deepest down ranch" in the country, it attracted many famous and important people: political leaders, wealthy business tycoons, artists, actors, writers, and those who wanted to get away from it all for a short time and enjoy the peace, calm, and beauty of the canyon. There were several individual cabins, a caretaker's cabin, and a combination recreation/dining hall that seated sixteen guests.

Time has brought changes to Phantom Ranch. It is no longer particularly exclusive, and it can now accommodate nearly one hundred people, plus more in the Bright Angel Campground. The Great Depression brought the first important changes when a Civilian Conservation Corps camp was established in the canyon. The CCC boys built trails, planted trees, graded the campground, and dug irrigation ditches. They also built a swimming pool, but this was filled up again in 1972 for sanitary reasons.

Today there are two ways to reach Phantom Ranch: one is by mule from the south rim, the other is on foot with a backpack from either rim. In any case, reservations should be made in advance—far in advance during the popular summer months. Usually there is a standby list of hopefuls waiting for a last minute cancellation. Spring or fall are probably the best times to make the trip. In summer, temperatures in the inner canyon can soar to well above 110 degrees, and in winter the wind is as cold as the icicles and ice sheets that hang from moist places on the upper canyon walls. The temperature is usually 20 degrees warmer at the bottom, but during winter, when the rim thermometer registers close to zero, the canyon bottom is also quite chilly.

There are advantages to the mule ride: at least the mule does all the work. "Be at the corral behind Bright Angel Lodge at 7:30 a.m.," are the instructions. So the riders appear and, once inside the circular stone corral, each is sized up by the head wrangler and assigned to a mule. Half-day and one-day riding groups go first; then, by 8:30 the first string of riders for Phantom Ranch moves out. Eight riders and a wrangler are off (but not running), and the second string begins to mount up.

Down the Bright Angel Trail they go, and the riders' legs, unaccustomed to the spread across a mule's broad back, get stiffer and stiffer. By box-lunch time at Indian Gardens, most riders are so stiff that the wrangler must help each to dismount. Most collapse into his arms, and all stagger awkwardly about until the circulation returns to their legs and feet.

Hikers can start whenever they like—daybreak or noon—just so they make their final destination before dark. They need to carry water (two quarts per day at least) and whatever food and camping gear they choose; a weekend backpacker may carry gear weighing from thirty to sixty pounds. On the trail the mules have the right of way so foot traffic is supposed to stand still and let them pass. Most hikers observe the rule; however, the trick is not to stop at a place where the mules have chosen to relieve themselves. They all use the same spot and the aroma is quite emphatic.

The mule strings reach Phantom Ranch by 2 or 3 o'clock in the afternoon. Riders are assigned their cabins and left to amuse themselves until supper time. Coffee, hot cocoa, and cold beer are available when the bar is open; the "bar" is the dining room and there is a closed spell for table setting between the last drink and the dinner call. Meals are served family style and a generous steak supper, lodging, and ample breakfast are included in the price of the trip.

Next morning the mules start out again at about 9 o'clock and return to the rim by way of the shorter, steeper South Kaibab Trail. There is no box lunch and no stop unless someone needs to use the open-to-the-sky john about two-thirds of the way up. At the top, usually by 1 o'clock, all riders are presented with a Master Mule Skinners certificate, complete with their name and date; then they are bused from Yaki Point back to Bright Angel Lodge.

As for the backpackers, when they reach the bottom they set up camp in the Bright Angel Campground. If they want to buy an evening meal in the ranch dining hall, they are fed a hearty supper of beef stew after the mule riders have finished. Hikers can stay longer than one night, so they have a chance to explore the canyon bottom. Hiking choices include the Phantom Ranch area (3.5 miles), the River Loop (1.5 miles), a full-day trip to Ribbon Falls (13 miles), or the overnight hike to Clear Creek (18 miles) for which a permit from the backcountry reservations office is required.

In the good old days when Phantom Ranch was more exclusive, guests who rode down could stay longer than one night to enjoy the isolation and savor the beauties of the canyon at their leisure. Nowadays, the only way to stay longer is to hike in and camp. The visitor who rides a mule down must ride back up the next day. To stay longer means paying for two trips because a mule must go down riderless in order to bring an extra rider back. Not many people choose to do that.

People who work at the ranch are the kind who enjoy solitude and isolation, and employees often stay for years because they like it there. Supplies come down once a week and everything has to be packed in by mule. In case of serious illness or injury, the patient has to be packed out. Clothes get well worn and do not have to be fancy. There is no television or movie, and radio reception is not too good; bird songs, or the chorus of frogs, crickets, and other insects are music enough for most.

Over the years since Mary Colter first designed it, Phantom Ranch has matured. Sometimes it is described as rustic and sometimes as antiquated or even shabby. Cottonwoods that were planted by the CCC boys have grown into great trees that tower over the low cabins and in autumn their fallen leaves make a thick carpet on the trails. Grass grows tall to hide the cabin foundations. The native stone buildings blend more than ever into their natural surroundings, just as their designer intended. Mary Elizabeth Jane Colter, artistic, imperious, demanding, as her contemporaries described her, would surely approve. The woman of the Grand Canyon left her mark.

The million-acre Grand Canyon Game Preserve, established in 1906, was home for some three thousand Rocky Mountain mule deer.

CHAPTER VI

CANYON CREATURES

ANIMALS HAVE BEEN AT HOME IN THE GRAND CANYON FOR MILLIONS OF YEARS. When ancient seas drained away, shells and fossil remains were left behind as sediments and formed the basis of the canyon rocks. Other creatures, long gone, left their tracks in soft places that have since become sandstone—they have given meaning to the metaphor, leaving footprints in the sands of time. During the last couple of million years, the canyon has influenced the lives and shapes of creatures living in or near it. It has also served as a roadblock to the movements of some of them.

Sheer cliffs, deep canyons, and a fast moving river are no obstacles to birds; they can fly over such barriers. For a time, though, it was believed that a cross-canyon flight might be too dangerous for a bird to undertake. Tricky air currents, downdrafts, and air pockets would pull even the strongest fliers, like eagles, owls, and hawks, down to their doom. Small birds, it was believed, could not possibly make such a hazardous journey. But then a red-backed junco—a gray and brown bird no bigger than a sparrow—spoiled this theory. The junco was released by the park's ranger-naturalist from a trap on the south rim on 16 December 1932 wearing band no. H–72850. That same small bird, still wearing its numbered band, walked into another naturalist's trap on the north rim on 20 April 1933. So much for the bird-destroying canyon air currents!

The same species of birds, and there are many of them, are found on both rims, as well as in the canyon itself. What makes the difference are the living conditions they prefer and the kinds of food they like. Eagles, owls, and hawks live where there are plenty of mice, rabbits, lizards, and other birds to prey on; seed-eaters are found where there are pine cones, seed-producing weeds, and such.

Of the reptiles, lizards enjoy the canyon paradise, but the snake population is not very large. The lizards are harmless, but the rattlesnakes can be dangerous if an unwary hiker is careless about foot or hand placement. Characteristically, the canyon has produced its own special subspecies of rattlesnake and, while anyone, anywhere, can see pink elephants if he drinks enough alcohol, only a cold-sober Grand Canyon visitor can see a pink rattlesnake. Believe it or not, the Grand Canyon rattlesnake, *(Crotalus viridis abyssus)* varies in color from vermillion to salmon pink with few other markings to mar its original pinkness.

The first of these pink rattlers was collected by park naturalist Edwin D. McKee along the Tanner Trail about three hundred feet below the south rim on a warm September morning in 1929. He was crossing a sunny stretch of white Kaibab limestone.

"In the middle of this white outcrop," McKee reported, "coiled like a rope and just as motionless, was a medium-sized salmon-pink rattlesnake which I noticed at once because of the contrast in color between it and the rock. It watched me intently but made no move other than a short warning rattle. Immediately I became intrigued with the idea that this colorful rattler was a variety that I had never seen before nor was I familiar with any published description of it. And it seemed clearly up to me, as park naturalist at Grand Canyon, to learn more about this specimen; it required collecting the snake alive in order not to injure the diagnostic scale pattern of its head.

"To capture the rattler was not difficult," he continued, "for I was familiar with the method of pinning down its head with a stick and grasping it by the neck directly behind. What I had not reckoned on, however, was the rather strenuous task ahead of me in transporting it out of the Canyon. I had no collecting sack so had to carry the snake out by hand, and the combination of a steep trail and the snake's dead weight (unlike many snakes, the rattler hangs straight and limp) created something of an undertaking.

"On top, my car was waiting among the trees and I had only to drive a few miles over a winding dirt road to the Desert View Ranger Station, where I could expect assistance in caging the specimen. This seemed a relatively easy task except, of course, I had to continue holding the snake in one hand while I drove with the other. I recall clearly that I was carrying the pink rattler in my right hand and reasoned that should I drop it for any reason while driving, it would be near my feet. Thus a transfer to my left hand had to be arranged. Finally, with the snake dangling out of the window, I drove in low gear to the station and arrived with my specimen conspicuously on display, much to the amazement of the local ranger."

Soon thereafter the pink rattlesnake was shipped by railway express to the San Diego Zoo. The snake expert there recognized it as a variety new to science. It was classified, officially named Grand Canyon rattlesnake, and made comfortable as a notable zoo resident.

Further studies have indicated that the pink snakes are found only inside the canyon. Their pink color matches the redwall areas of the canyon so they are not easily seen. Apparently the snakes are satisfied with their super camouflage; they are not aggressive, and hikers who meet any of the pink individuals will find the snake willing to leave them alone if they do the same for it.

Noted hiker and author Colin Fletcher described the pink specimens he saw as "gentlemanly." In his book *The Man Who Walked Through Time,* Fletcher tells of sitting on a sandbank at the edge of the Colorado watching

a pale-pink rattlesnake come gliding over the sand, barely six feet away from me. I felt curiosity rather than fear. The snake was clearly unaware of my presence. Slowly, gracefully, it threaded its way through a forest of willow shoots. As its flank passed each stem I could see the individual scales tilt under the stem's pressure, then move back flush. Four feet from my left buttock the snake stopped, its head in a sun-dappled patch of sand beside a cluster of roots. Unhurriedly, it drew its body forward and curled into a flat resting coil. Then it stretched and yawned. It yawned a long and unmistakable yawn. A yawn so uninhibited that for many slow seconds I seemed to see nothing but the pale lining of its mouth and two matching arcs of small, sharp teeth. When the yawn was over at last, the snake raised its head and twisted it slowly and luxuriously from side to side, as a man or woman will do in anticipation of rest and comfort to come. Finally, with such obvious contentment that I do not think I would have been surprised to hear the creature purr, it laid its head gently on the pillow of its clean and beautifully marked body.

After watching all this, Fletcher found himself "feeling for it something remarkably close to affection."

The pink canyon rattlesnake is a relative of the Arizona prairie rattlesnake, found in desert areas south of the canyon and used by the Hopi Indians in their famous snake dances.

The Grand Canyon also has played a part in the lives and development of some of the seventy-four different kinds of mammals that live along its edges. Eleven different species of them are found only on the north rim, and fourteen species are found only on the south rim. The canyon itself is enough of a barrier to block their spread. Twelve species of mammals found on both rims are different enough in small but important details to be classified as separate subspecies on the north and on the south.

The most outstanding example of the canyon's influence is shown by two squirrel cousins, the Abert squirrel on the south rim and the Kaibab squirrel on the north rim. Both are large squirrels with thick, bushy tails. In winter, they grow inch-long tufts of hair on the tips of their ears and for this reason they are called tassel-eared squirrels. Their living and eating habits are similar; the main difference between them is their color, for the Abert is white underneath with a silver-gray tail, while the Kaibab is black underneath with a white tail.

The dark Kaibabs are more shy than their gray relatives. They are found only on the north rim in an area not larger than thirty by seventy miles, most of it inside the boundaries of Grand Canyon National Park. The Aberts, on the other hand, are found only on the south rim, although their range also includes parts of northern Arizona and New Mexico, southern Utah and Nevada, and parts of the Sierra Madre in northern Mexico.

The explanation, some scientists think, is that a small group of Abert squirrels managed, somehow, to get across the canyon about two million years ago (it was not so wide then). After that big effort, the travelers were content to settle down and stay put, slowly developing colors different from their cousins. Whatever the case, the stay-at-home Kaibabs enjoy a claim to widespread fame because they have concentrated their efforts on becoming different from their south-rim cousins.

Another kind of animal on the north rim gained international fame because it was starving to death. This was the mule deer, which is found on both rims and down in the canyon. It was the Kaibab herd that had the food problems. The difficulty began in 1906 when President Theodore Roosevelt signed the bill that created the Grand Canyon Game Preserve. This million-acre area of the Kaibab Plateau was home for some three thousand Rocky Mountain mule deer. They were fine animals and the bucks wore magnificent antlers, but they were not alone on the range. Thousands of domestic cattle, sheep, and horses from big ranches in southern Utah and northern Arizona Territory were also pastured on the Kaibab. With all of these animals competing for grazeland, the food supply was soon limited and the land began to show all the bad effects of over-grazing.

In earlier times, natural predators like mountain lions, wolves, bobcats, and coyotes, as well as large birds of prey, kept the deer population fairly constant. But after forest rangers and professional hunters killed off most of the predators "to protect the deer," the situation changed. By 1924, having few natural enemies to check them, there were somewhere between twenty thousand and fifty thousand deer in the herd, producing four to six thousand additional fawns every year. All those deer, plus the domestic cattle, needed more food than the land could provide. Grass was eaten to the roots, bushes were eaten back to nubs, leaves and branches were stripped from trees as far up as a hungry deer could reach. Winter came and thousands of deer starved, but by spring there was a new crop of fawns to make up for the losses.

Something had to be done to save both the range and the deer. Zane Grey, the western novelist, leading citizens of Flagstaff, and various sportsmen's organizations became interested; they financed George McCormick of Flagstaff to organize a super deer drive. His plan was to drive no less than three thousand and no more than eight thousand deer from the Kaibab, down through Nankoweap Canyon, across the Colorado, and up the Tanner Trail to better range on the south rim. He was to collect $2.50 for every deer delivered.

The day selected for the drive was 16 December 1924, and early on that cold winter morning 125 men, including seventy Navajo Indians, were in line, on foot, and on horseback. They had tin cans to pound on, cow bells to ring, plus any other kind of noise-maker they could think of. With a yell and a bang the drive started. Trouble was inevitable because deer do not drive like cattle. A storm came up, some of the drivers were scattered, and a few of them became lost. Startled deer broke through and around the line of remaining cowboys and raced back to their home range, hungrier than ever. Not a single deer was chased across the river.

The problem was eventually solved by increased hunting, systematic reduction of deer numbers, and cattle reduction on the range. But before that was finally accomplished, the state of Arizona and the National Forest Service got into a debate over hunting permits that went all the way to the United States Supreme Court. The Supreme Court finally ruled against the state. Now, by various methods, the deer population in the Kaibab Forest, which extends into the north rim of the park, is maintained at a level that fits the food supply. But a lot of deer had to starve to death before people—conservationists, foresters, cattlemen, and hunters—learned to fit the number of deer to the carrying capacity of the land.

Another canyon oddity, this one in the Colorado River, is the world's largest minnow. In the early days of sport fishing, specimens of this minnow reportedly weighed almost one hundred pounds and measured nearly six feet long. Fishermen called it a Colorado squawfish or white salmon. Scientists called it *Ptychocheilus lucius* and, because of certain physical characteristics, they classified it as a minnow. This giant minnow liked the deep, swift water of the undammed river and swam upstream to spawn in some of the shallower creeks. Glen Canyon Dam has caused changes in river depth, current, and water temperature, and these changes have profoundly affected the habitat of the fish. The Colorado squawfish is definitely an endangered species.

Also approaching the endangered stage are several other Colorado River fish including the humpback chub, the bonytail chub, and the razorback sucker. Their econiches in the colder, clearer water below the dams are being taken over by stock fish such as trout, catfish, crappie, and bass. Fishermen, for the most part, approve of these newer sport-type species; as for the native fish, it is likely that the endangered status will stick, as non-native species are introduced and natural habitat is changed or destroyed.

In addition to the many real birds, mammals, and reptiles that live on its rims and in its depths, the Grand Canyon also supports a number of unreal creatures that are the products of many fertile imaginations. Earliest of these on record is the Hydrophobic Skunk, first reported by Irvin S. Cobb in 1913. Apparently the skunk was well established by that time and it made quite an impression on Mr. Cobb because he described it in two different places in his book *Roughing It De Luxe*.

According to Cobb, the Hydrophobic Skunk lived only at the extreme bottom of the canyon and was so rare that only natives of the area had ever seen it. Tourists had never met it, although many tourists met other tourists who had met other people (natives, probably) who had seen the creature.

Besides having the equipment of the ordinary skunk, the Hydrophobic Skunk, Cobb said, "is rabid in the most rabidissimus form. He is not just mad part of the time, like one's relatives by marriage—and not mad most of the time, like a railroad ticket agent—but mad all the time—incurably, enthusiastically and unanimously mad! He is mad and he is glad of it."

Later, when Cobb and a friend rode muleback down to the bottom of the canyon and spent the night there, he learned more about the unusual skunk from his two cowboy guides, Johnny and Bill. In cowboy lingo they called the creatures Hydrophobys. New moons brought the creatures out, the cowboys said, and, oddly enough, it happened to be new moon the night Cobb and his friend were in the canyon.

"The Hydrophobys usually travel in pairs," Johnny said. "You'd know one the minute you saw him though," Bill added. "They're smaller than a regular skunk and spotted where the other kind is striped. And they got little red eyes. You won't have no trouble at all recognizin' one."

To this, Johnny added the information that the Hydrophobys were mad—born that way. As for being dangerous to humans, he added, "Why humans is their favorite pastime! Humans is just pie to a Hydrophoby Skunk. It ain't really any fun to be bit by a Hydrophoby Skunk neither."

Bill agreed to this and added his contribution. "They aim to catch you asleep and creep right up soft and take holt of you—take holt of a year usually—and clamp their teeth and just hang on for further orders. Some say they hang on 'till it thunders, same as snappin' turtles. But that's a lie, I judge, because there's weeks on a stretch down here by the rapids when it don't thunder. All the cases I ever heard of they let go at sun-up."

"It is right painful at the time," Johnny took up the thread of the story, "and then in nine days you go mad yourself. Remember that fellow the Hydrophoby Skunk bit down here by the rapids, Bill? Let's see now—what was that man's name?"

"Williams," supplied Bill. "Heck Williams. I saw him at Flagstaff when they took him there to the hospital. That guy certainly did carry on regardless. First he went mad and his eyes turned red, and he got so he didn't have no real use for water—well, them prospectors don't never care much about water anyway—and then he got to snappin' and bitin' and foamin' so's they had to strap him down to his bed. He got loose, though."

"Broke loose, I suppose?" Cobb said, to keep the story going. "No, he bit loose," said Bill with the air of one who would not deceive you even in a matter of small details. "Do you mean to say he bit those leather straps in two?" Cobb questioned further. "No, sir; he couldn't reach them," explained Bill, "so he bit the bed in two. Not in one bite, of course," he went on. "It took several. I saw him after he was laid out. He really wasn't no credit to himself as a corpse."

That night Cobb and friend had some difficulty in getting to sleep. Later, when they did drop off, a pack rat invaded their tent and it set off a wild alarm. Next morning Bill and Johnny did a lot of laughing between themselves after breakfast, but neither Cobb nor his friend thought to ask why.

Another creature said to exist in the remote regions of the canyon is the Pygmy Horse. It is supposed to be no bigger than a dog, and while accounts from the canyon are vague, some carnivals and circuses have shown dog-sized horses and claimed they came from the Grand Canyon in Arizona.

Scientists are unsure, but perhaps there is a chance that an ancient ancestor of the horse—a dog-sized creature called *Eohippus* or Dawn Horse, which became extinct some thirty-five million years ago—might have survived on some isolated mesa in the canyon. This theory became more widespread after a motion picture called *The Lost World* was made in the early 1930s. In it, scientists found real dinosaurs still living on a remote plateau in South America. So why not Pygmy Horses in the Grand Canyon?

Shiva Temple, a large, flat-topped mesa in the canyon, was selected as the logical place for the little horses to survive. It was big enough, supported a forested area of comfortable size, had sheer walls that were thought to be unclimbable, and had been cut off from the rest of the Kaibab Plateau for thousands of years. In 1937, a scientist from the American Museum of Natural History decided to climb the mesa and see. Newspapers caught wind of the project, and the story made front pages all over the world.

Logically, Emery Kolb, the canyon photographer, was the best person to guide the expedition, but the eastern scientists ignored local talent and chose someone else instead. Scorned and rejected, Emery climbed Shiva Temple twice before the museum people got there and was careful to leave evidence behind him. When the easterners finally reached the top, what did they find? Newly shed deer horns, some ancient pottery shards, and wrappings from Eastman-Kodak film. So much for Shiva Temple's isolation! Needless to say, there were no Pygmy Horses on the mesa; there was nothing living there that was any different from other life forms in the rest of the canyon.

When raft trips down the Colorado became popular, they spawned a new breed of tall-tale tellers in the men and women who pilot the rafts; they have created a whole new zoo of canyon creatures. Most elaborate of these are the Woollywookses, whose tale is best told somewhere between Badger Creek and Soap Creek rapids. It was the Woollywookses—along with the Sierra Club and other conservation groups—who kept the federal government from building Marble Canyon Dam.

Woollywookses are pretty creatures, covered with soft, yellow fur. They are so small that it would take two thousand of their skins to make one mini-coat, without sleeves, that is. With sleeves it would take 750 more. Their favorite food is iron and they were especially fond of old fashioned beer cans, the kind prospectors and miners used to toss in the river or leave lying around their camps.

When government engineers came into Marble Canyon with their metal surveying tools, their iron rods to mark out dam foundations, steel cables, pipes, and other equipment, the Woollywookses had a feast. Any sledge hammer, iron pipe, or pile of steel rods left out overnight were promptly eaten down to the last rust spots by hungry Woollywookses. They even ate the metal barges that engineers used to cross the river.

Finally, the engineers had to give up. They collected what was left of their gear and went back to Washington, D.C., to tell the secretary of the interior that a dam could not be built in Marble Canyon. The same thing happened to the proposed Bridge Canyon Dam.

Woollywookses are gentle little creatures and it is fairly easy to trap them. To do this, a person need only to go out at dusk and bury a series of iron beer cans up to their rims along the river, leaving just a little beer in the bottom of each can. Next morning the Woollywookses will be so full of iron and beer that they cannot run away. Only the male Woollywookses drink, of course, but the females are too loyal to desert their mates so they, too, are captured.

Lately, though, the river pilot laments, Woollywookses have become very scarce—in fact, they may be extinct. The reason is that most, if not all, of the beer companies have switched from iron to aluminum cans, and the little creatures are starving to death.

Farther on, where the canyon walls have become higher and more jagged, the pilot will point to an opening in one of the frowning cliffs. "That's the kind of place to find an Owlogorpion nest," he says. "Owlogorpions have to back into their nests and they like crooked-shaped caves so their tails will fit."

Owlogorpions, he further explains, are hybrids found only in the Grand Canyon. They are a cross between a southern Utah hoot owl and a northern Arizona scorpion. They are rarely seen because they fly mainly at night. This is a good thing because an Owlogorpion can be dangerous; it can bite with its owl-like beak and sting with its scorpion tail all at the same time.

What do Owlogorpions eat? Well, Rock Squirrels, mainly, but they are not above robbing nests of Gosh Hawks and Golly Eagles that also live in cracks and crannies in the canyon walls. This explanation leads to more canyon unnatural history.

Gosh Hawks are much like regular hawks, except that their wings make a "gosh, gosh, gosh" sound when the wind whistles through their partly petrified feathers. And why are their feathers petrified? That is because the Gosh Hawks swallow so much silt along with the fish they catch from the muddy Colorado River that their wing feathers have sandstone tips.

Another story about Gosh Hawks tells how Major John Wesley Powell named them during his 1869 voyage through the canyon. One day while Powell was eating his lunch and taking notes at the same time, which was a difficult task for a one-armed man, some birds flew overhead, and the men asked Powell what kind they were. The major was so busy taking notes and worrying about the birds stealing his food that he did not hear their inquiry. Instead, he looked up suddenly and mumbled, "Oh, my gosh, hawks!" The men were satisfied, and the birds have been called Gosh Hawks ever since.

The Golly Eagles get their name from eastern visitors who, upon seeing one of them soaring majestically above the canyon, are certain to exclaim, "Golly, look at the Eagle!"

High up along the canyon edge, especially on the north rim, a visitor with a good pair of field glasses can sometimes catch sight of a rare Goatalope—a cross between a Rocky Mountain goat and a pronghorn antelope. These creatures have lived for so many generations on the edge of the Grand Canyon that their legs grow longer on one side than on the other. Goatalopes can run swiftly along the canyon rim, but once away from the edge they are easily captured; because of their uneven legs, they can only run in circles.

Another creature, the rarest of all, is the Crockagator, which lives in the depths of the muddy Colorado. The creature has a crocodile head on one end of its body and an alligator head on the other end. The reptile has many digestive problems and suffers from chronic constipation; it is little wonder the Crockagator has such a mean disposition.

Entertainment at the canyon is easily provided by stories old and new. Storytelling has become a lost art in this day of television and radio, but in the isolation available in the depths of the canyon, the art is very much alive. Long may it flourish, and may many more creatures be invented along the Colorado River.

In Granite Gorge below Sockdolager Rapid, December 1911. The Colorado River rarely discloses its many mysteries.

CHAPTER VII

CANYON MYSTERIES

THE GRAND CANYON HOLDS MANY MYSTERIES, AND THE COLORADO RIVER RARELY gives up any of its victims. Occasionally, however, one of the mysteries is solved and some long lost victim—usually in the form of weathered bones—comes to light. One of the most intriguing mysteries of the canyon is the identity of the first Euro-American to venture into its depths and live to tell the story, or at least to leave some evidence that someone had been there.

It is generally agreed that Major John Wesley Powell and the men who accompanied him on his 1869 trip through the canyon were the first to officially explore it. That is what the Powell Monument says:

> Major John Wesley Powell
> first explorer of the Grand Canyon
> descended the river in row boats
> traversing the gorge beneath this point
> Aug. 17, 1869 and again Sept. 1, 1872.

Major Powell officially explored the canyon, but was he the first man to go through it?

Carved into the canyon walls at five different places is the name "D. Julien" and the date 1836. Frederick Dellenbaugh reported seeing the name first in

Labyrinth Canyon when he was with Major Powell's 1872 expedition. A few years later the Stanton surveying party found two additional places where D. Julien had carved his name; prospectors found two more, making a total of five. Three of the inscriptions gave the name and year only, but two had day dates also: "3 Mai" and "16 Mai." The "3 Mai" was twenty miles farther downstream than the date recorded thirteen days later. Stanton reported that the May third carving was high up on a rock wall under an overhanging cliff where it could only have been made from a boat during fairly high water. Near it on the same rock was a crude picture of a boat; it was assumed that the inscription and the picture were done by the same person. Located near the end of Cataract Canyon, the inscriptions are now covered by the water of Lake Powell.

Who was the mysterious D. Julien and what was he doing in the canyon thirty-three years before the first Powell expedition? Why was the earlier date farther down the river than the later one? Were they carved at the same time or on separate trips? Was he a trapper following trails down to the river at various places or was he in a boat braving the perils of the Colorado?

Dellenbaugh tried to solve the mystery before his book *A Canyon Voyage* was published. Thinking that D. Julien might have been a Catholic missionary, he wrote to the Vatican in Rome, but the records there made no mention of such a person. The mystery was as dark as ever and it remained so for many years.

In 1931, a professor from the University of Utah, while waiting for the start of the Sun Dance on the Uintah Indian Reservation, did some exploring. On a bluff near the Uintah River he found a place where many early travelers had carved their names and among them was "Denis Julien, 1831." The canyon mystery man had surfaced again, but this date was five years earlier than his canyon carvings. Still, it was a clue, for it was known that French traders had been in the area in 1831. Records of their activities could be found in the Missouri Historical Library in St. Louis. Would D. Julien be among them? More research unearthed the baptismal records of three of Denis Julien's children and the burial record of one child. There were also two permits of Julien's for trade with the Indians registered in the Superintendency of Louisiana, and one order for "358 barrels of lead"; the Indians needed lead to make bullets. Julien and his brother Etienne had also volunteered for service in a Louisiana artillery company in 1809.

At least a part of the puzzle was solved. D. Julien was a French-Canadian trader and trapper who may have gone into the Utah area in 1831 with a larger group organized by the Robidoux brothers in search of trade and beaver skins. The carvings he made along the Colorado in 1836 are the last records of him. By that time he must have been in his sixties; his children were born in the late 1790s. The rapids below his inscription at the end of Cataract Canyon were dangerous ones, so another uncertainty remains. Did D. Julien try to run those rapids in his boat and become the first pioneer casualty of the river? That is mystery number one.

The second mystery involves a man who may have gone through the canyon in the summer of 1867, two years ahead of Powell. He lived to tell about it, but not everybody believed his story. Even today there are those who do and those who do not; it is still possible to get up a heated argument about it.

The man was James White. He drifted into the scene on a small raft at the frontier outpost of Callville, [Nevada] on the Colorado River the afternoon of 8 September 1867. He was thin, sun-blistered, battered, scratched, and bruised; his hair and beard were long and bleached; he wore only a shirt and coat, both of them tattered and water-worn. He was conscious but weak from hunger and somewhat confused. The man who pulled him ashore thought he was on the edge of insanity. With rest, food, and the care available on the frontier, James White was soon able to tell a story that for danger and adventure can have little competition.

In April of 1867, with three other men, White had set out from Fort Dodge, Kansas, on a prospecting trip. One man dropped out because of a gunshot wound in the foot, but the other three continued on, prospecting along the way until they reached the Grand River. High cliffs kept them away from water until they found a side canyon that they followed down to the river. They camped for the night of 23 August and next morning they started back up the canyon. At that point Indians attacked them and their leader, Captain Baker, was killed. As White later described it, "The Indians were hiding behind the rocks overlooking the canyon. Baker expired shortly after the fatal shot, and, much to our grief, we had to leave his remains, as the Indians were close upon us; and George Stroll and I had to make our escape as soon as possible, going back down the canyon. We left our horses in the brush and we took our overcoats, lariats, guns, ammunition, and 1 quart of flour, and I also had a knife scabbard made out of rawhide, and I also had a knife, and we started afoot down the canyon."

When they reached the river they made a raft of logs tied together with their lariats and after dark they set out, poling their way downstream with the current. Next day they passed the mouth of the San Juan River and floated smoothly on for three days. Each day they mixed a little flour with water and drank it.

"On the third day, about 5 o'clock, we went over a rapid," White later recalled, "and George got washed off, but I caught hold of him and got him back on the raft again." The rapid also soaked their remaining flour, so they scraped it off the sack and ate it. That was the last of their food supply. The current carried them on, and the walls of the canyon closed in, rising, White estimated, from two to three thousand feet above them. On the fourth day they rebuilt their raft, making it larger and stronger, but the next whirlpool washed George overboard again, and this time he disappeared forever.

White drifted on, tying himself to the raft to make sure he did not suffer his companion's fate. On and on he drifted, passing the mouth of the Little Colorado River, where a whirlpool spun him around for several hours. Then on again, over four or five rapids until night, when he rested against the rock wall with his raft securely tied against the current.

On the sixth day he gathered a handful of mesquite beans from a bush on an island and ate them. There were many, many more rapids on the seventh, eighth, ninth, and tenth days, but no food. With nothing else to eat, he cut his rawhide knife scabbard into small pieces and swallowed them. On the eleventh day he went over a big rapid, lying flat on his raft and hanging on for dear life. On the twelfth day his raft was washed onto some rocks and he could not get it off, so he built a smaller raft and started on again by moonlight. About dawn he saw some Indians along the shore and they gave him some mesquite bread to eat. But they also stole his half-axe and one of his revolvers, and they tore his coat, trying to pull it off of him.

Back on his raft, he floated on until afternoon when he came upon another band of Indians. With these he traded his remaining revolver and vest for the skinned hindquarters of a dog. He ate half of the meat for supper, roasting it on the coals.

"The Indians being afraid of me," he concluded his story, "drove me out of their camp, and I retreated to the bank of the river that night, and in the morning, the fourteenth day after I got on my raft, I started to eat the other quarter, but I dropped it in the water. I floated on that day until 3 o'clock and landed at Callville, and a man came out and pulled me ashore."

White's story was published in various newspapers, but in 1867 on the western frontier news did not travel very fast nor spread very widely. White recovered, worked for awhile in Callville and then moved on. He cut ties for the railroad, hired out as wagon boss, ran a saloon, drove stage, ran a stage station, and finally in 1878 he drifted to Trinidad, Colorado, where he settled down. He raised a family and spent the rest of his life in Trinidad as a hard-working, honest, respected citizen. A number of his friends willingly testified to that effect when the story of his Colorado River adventure was attacked.

And attacked James White's story was, especially after Major Powell made his trips through the canyon. No one, it was charged, could have lived through the journey that James White described. Fourteen days was too short a time to travel the distance he claimed—from above the San Juan to Callville, a matter of some five hundred miles. There was no whirlpool where the Little Colorado joined the main river. The canyon walls are a thousand or more feet higher than White said they were, and he described them as "white sandstone"; rather, they are limestone, stained red by iron deposits from the layers above.

In defense, it was pointed out that he could have traveled five hundred miles in fourteen days pushed by a river current varying from calm to roaring rapids, and with no time out for rest, relaxation, eating, or comfortable camping. There may have been a whirlpool where he said there was because currents change from time to time. As for the walls, he might have underestimated their height and even their color. After all, he was struggling to stay alive and was not making scientific observations.

Did White "pitch a yarn" and concoct "one of the best bits of fiction" as Frederick Dellenbaugh claimed? Was he mistaken about where his trip on the river began? Or did he tell the truth about one of the wildest adventures a man could survive? Were Major Powell's friends reluctant to admit that anyone could have gone down the river before him? Chalk up another mystery for the Grand Canyon.

The next mystery concerns Glen and Bessie Hyde, a young, newly married couple from Idaho. They decided to spend their honeymoon running the Colorado River in the fall of 1928.

Glen was a tall, slender, earnest looking young man of twenty-eight, and Bessie was a small, ninety-pound woman of twenty-four years. A photograph of them standing together near Kolb Studio on the south rim shows that she came only to her husband's shoulder. The trip was probably his idea; he looks much more outdoorsy than she does.

To prepare for the trip the Hydes built their own boat at Green River, Utah. It was an open, blunt-ended scow, twenty feet long, five feet wide, and three feet deep, with a sweep oar at either end. It was a clumsy looking craft quite different from the decked or open rowboat types usually used by river runners.

They left Green River on 20 October and twenty-six days later reached Bright Angel Creek. Leaving their scow tied to the river bank they hiked up the trail to visit Emery Kolb, who was shocked to learn that the Hydes were not wearing life preservers on the river and offered them the use of his. When they refused, he tried to persuade them to take along some inner tubes, but they only looked at each other and smiled, saying they were both good swimmers and such things were unnecessary.

Later, Emery recalled that Bessie Hyde did not seem very eager to continue the trip. Twice already, she told him, Glen had been thrown into the river and both times she had barely managed to get a rope to him. Looking at Kolb's daughters's shoes, Bessie said, "I wonder if I shall ever wear pretty shoes again." Next day they hiked back down the trail and were never seen again.

When the couple did not reach the end of their trip on schedule, Hyde's father began a search. An army plane from March Air Base was sent to help. It was the first plane to venture into the inner gorge, and the pilot sighted the scow about fourteen miles below the mouth of Diamond Creek. The Kolbs—Ellsworth had come from Los Angeles to help in the search—and Chief Ranger Jim Brooks reached the Hydes' craft on 1 December. It was floating right side up with about fourteen inches of water in the bottom. Both oars were in place and a dragging rope was caught on rocks in deep water. Glen's gun was there, along with Bessie's camera and notebook. The Kolbs' book about the river, which the couple had been using as a guide, was open on the seat.

Hyde's father searched along the shore and found the couple's tracks about seven miles above Diamond Creek, and farther down Glen's were found along a rapid. They led to the river and did not return.

What happened to the bride and groom remains a mystery. Emery Kolb had his own theory, based on what he knew of the couple's usual plan of action. Bessie would stand on the bank holding the scow's rope while Glen walked ahead to examine the next rapid. Possibly she had been pulled or blown into the river—the weather was squally—he jumped in to save her, and the Colorado claimed them both. The rapid at mile 232 is a nasty one and that may have been where the accident happened. The scow floated on for five miles until its trailing rope caught on the rocks and held it. But only the Colorado River knows what really happened to that young Idaho couple who never finished their honeymoon.

Bert Loper's story is unusual because, after twenty-six years, the mystery of Bert's disappearance may have been solved. But, meanwhile, Bert Loper has become a part of canyon folklore, a ghostly figure rowing a ghostly boat on a darkened river, or prowling camps and playing tricks on sleeping river runners.

Like many other men before and after him, Albert (Bert) Loper was charmed by the spell of the canyon and the river. He began on the San Juan River in 1893–94, and by 1907 he was prospecting and "running" on the Colorado. The river had a fascination that held him to it for half a century before finally taking Bert forever. Sometimes he made it through the canyon successfully; sometimes his boat was wrecked or damaged so that he could not continue. But back again he would go, and in 1939 his name was listed among the first hundred to successfully run the canyon.

Sometimes Bert went alone; other times he was a guide or chief boatman for scientific expeditions. His years of accumulated experience gave him a tremendous knowledge of the canyons and rapids of the Colorado and its tributaries: the

Green, the Yampa, the Grand, the Gunnison, and the San Juan. He shared his notes, advice, and recommendations for boat improvements with other river runners, and this gave him status as dean of the river runners. As the years passed, he became widely known as the "Grand Old Man of the Colorado."

Ill health and a bad gall bladder slowed him down somewhat, but as his eightieth birthday approached, Bert was determined to spend it on his beloved river. In preparation, he spent the winter of 1948–49 building a special plywood boat for the trip, a boat he named the *Grand Canyon*. His birthday was 31 July, and on 7 July 1949, he started from Lee's Ferry on his final trip. With him was a passenger, Wayne Nichol, two other boats, and a neoprene raft. The next day, at mile 24.5, the *Grand Canyon* capsized. Nichol made it to shore, but Bert was last seen floating with the current ahead of his overturned boat. No one knew for sure whether he drowned or had a heart attack.

The next afternoon his boat was found lodged on a rocky bar near the right bank at mile 41.5. Friends pulled it up on shore, well above the high water mark, and left it there. On the front deck they painted the epitaph:

Bert Loper
The Grand Old Man of the Colorado
Born July 31, 1869   Died July 8, 1949
Near Mile 25

No trace of Bert was found. Years passed and his boat remained on the shore, its plywood sides getting more warped and weathered with the passage of time. It survived the Colorado flood and high water in the summer of 1983, but friends know it cannot last forever. Many hope that the battered wreck will be moved to a museum of river lore before weather, time, and souvenir hunters have picked it completely to pieces.

Stories of Bert's exploits live on and slowly the river runners have woven them into folklore. Bert's ghost, they say, still roams the Colorado, sometimes angry at the increase of travel on his river. He haunts camp areas and causes numerous small annoyances. If a coffee pot tips over, if a raft's motor chokes and stalls, if some equipment turns up missing, there is one sure explanation: Bert Loper is responsible.

At night, if one listens carefully, above the roar of the river it is possible to sometimes hear a ghostly noise: creak-thump, creak-thump, creak-thump. It is the sound of wooden oars against metal oarlocks. Bert Loper is out rowing his boat, annoying rafters and collecting their equipment. Bert Loper has become the Davy Jones of the Colorado.

But occasionally the Colorado reveals one of its secrets and perhaps it has done so with Bert Loper. On 2 April 1975, a hiker from Socorro, New Mexico, reported to park rangers that he had found some human bones in the depths of the canyon at Cardenas Creek. They were below Lava Falls at an old high water mark seventy-five yards from the river on the south bank. Next day the Coconino County sheriff and a park ranger, using a helicopter, recovered the bones: skull, lower jawbone, pelvic bones, arm bones, and several vertebrae. The skull had not been damaged.

In the old days, bones like these would have been quietly buried in the canyon cemetery under a marker reading "Unknown." But with modern scientific methods, identification is often possible. Anthropologists at Northern Arizona University determined that the bones came from a man the same general size and age as Bert Loper. The brows were heavy, the nose unusual, and the jawbones showed that the skull's owner, like Bert, had been toothless for a long time before death. Other indications showed that the bones had lain exposed to the weather for between fifteen and twenty-five years.

As further evidence, a scientist skilled in anthropometry (the technique of human body measurement) sketched in a reconstruction of the face. The sketch was shown to a man who had known Loper and his comment was, "Yep, that's Bert."

A nephew was found and at his request the bones were buried beside the grave of Bert's wife in the Valley Cemetery at Sandy, Utah. Perhaps Bert would have preferred to remain beside his beloved Colorado River, but his ghost can remain—at least in folklore—and roam the canyon forever. And so ends another Colorado River mystery.

Rafters pause for a break in the canyon's inner gorge.

CHAPTER VIII

RIVER RATS,
A SPECIAL SUBSPECIES

THE RIVER RAT *(HOMO SAPIENS RIVERENSIS)* IS A COMPARATIVELY NEW SUBSPECIES, not yet fully classified by scientists, but found in ever-increasing numbers on the Colorado River within the confines of the Grand Canyon. River Rats are also found on other streams where there are rapids and thrills, such as the Green River in Utah and the Snake River in Idaho. They are most numerous, however, on the Colorado.

River Rats are creatures of greater interest to psychologists than to biologists because they are a breed set apart from normal human beings. They derive pleasure from being wet, scared, too cold or too hot, muddy, sandy, sunburned, and sometimes mosquito-bitten. They pay as much for a week of Spartan essentials as they would for a luxury vacation. They eat with their fingers, drink from tin cups, and sleep soundly on beds of sand or river gravel. At night, flashlight, firelight, and starlight are their only illumination, and in the event of rain, a tarp or a poncho is their only shelter. Nonetheless, the River Rat is a very special subspecies of the human animal.

To be exact, a River Rat is someone who has run the rapids of the Colorado (or other river) in a boat or raft for no other purpose than to say he/she has done it, and to experience the thrills and dangers that necessarily accompany river running. First evolving about A.D. 1938, River Rats can now be counted in the thousands.

Only recently has river running for sport become popular. After Major Powell and his crew made the first trip through the canyon in 1869, it was a full eighty years before one hundred people could claim to have done the same. Of the first hundred, beginning with Powell and the five men who made the full trip with him, eight were women. The first two female River Rats were Dr. Elzada Clover and Lois Jotter, botanists, who were members of a Norman Nevills expedition in 1938. Nevills was the first person to offer commercial trips through the canyon in specially designed cataract boats.

Like Powell, the earliest canyon travelers were there for a definite purpose: to examine the possibilities of a railroad, to prospect for minerals, to hunt and trap, to map the river, or to mark certain historic sites. But after 1927, the important work had been done and river running was on its way to becoming a major form of exciting outdoor recreation.

Some members of the first hundred managed to set records that have never been surpassed. Others who might have been included were drowned or gave up before the trip was completed. Earliest among those setting records was Nathaniel T. Galloway, who demonstrated in 1897 that it was better for a boat to go through a rapid stern first. That way, the person at the oars could see where the boat was going and avoid some of the rocks and other potential dangers. After Galloway, most of the runners adopted his technique and also faced downstream. In the winter of 1911–12, the Kolb brothers ran the river and made the first motion picture of river running so the less-venturesome canyon visitors could see what it was like to ride the rapids. In 1937, Haldane "Buzz" Holmstrom, rowing a boat of his own construction, made it alone through the canyon from Green River, Wyoming, to Hoover Dam. In 1938, Amos Berg ran the first inflatable raft through the canyon, pioneering the way for many such rafts to follow.

Clyde Eddy did not set any records, but the river trip he organized in 1927 was an odd one. Eddy, a journalist who wanted to run the Colorado, advertised in college newspapers and fraternity magazines for "geology students or young members of teaching faculties, to do field work in virgin territory." He got more than a hundred answers, but many applicants dropped out when they learned what the real project was.

When Eddy finally got his party organized, it included eight college students: three men from Harvard, two from Coe, two from Notre Dame, and one from Northwestern. There was also a young man from Louisiana, a news-reel cameraman, a Green River guide, and a hobo who happened by at the last minute and asked for a job. Added to these were an Airedale terrier named Rags, requisitioned from the Salt Lake City pound, and a bear cub (later named Cataract because he was so rough) bought in New York and taken west as a "picturesque" addition to the expedition.

Only the Green River guide had any experience with river running, but Eddy was convinced that "pink wristed" young college men could easily rise to meet any emergency. It was a rough trip, and by the time they reached Lee's Ferry two of the Harvard men, the cameraman, and the hobo were glad to leave the expedition.

The others, plus the dog and the bear, made it through to Needles, California, after a rugged six-week struggle. Everybody was glad the trip was over and they quickly went their separate ways. One of the college men took Rags home with him, while the bear cub was sold to a Santa Fe Railroad engineer bound for San Francisco. Eddy, the journalist, went east to write a book about the trip entitled *Down the World's Most Dangerous River*. The title was something of an exaggeration, but the book sold well and went into several editions.

River runners who followed the first one hundred set other records. In 1951, Jim and Bob Riggs rowed a Nevills cataract boat through the canyon in two and one-half days. In 1955, Bill Beer and John Daggett floated through the canyon without any kind of a boat or raft. Instead, they used GI neoprene packs as water wings.

In the summer of 1955, a new phenomenon appeared on the scene in the person of Georgie White, the only woman outfitter on the river. She was the first to take large parties (thirty at one time) through the canyon on World War II army surplus rubber rafts. She pioneered the technique of tying several rafts together and adding an outboard motor to give the mass more speed and better steering power.

Georgie's expeditions were organized on a "share the expense" plan. She furnished the food and rafts, but her passengers brought their own sleeping bags, gear, and whatever "luxuries" they could tuck into thirty pounds of luggage. People also were expected to help load and unload the rafts, make and break camp, and do other chores. It was Georgie White who gave the name of Royal River Rats to her through-the-canyon passengers. Other outfitters have come and gone or remained over the years, but for three decades Georgie White has continued to be "Woman of the River."

Why do people want to run the river? Probably "because it is there." But more than that, a trip through the rapids of the Colorado is never to be forgotten and probably never to be equaled. It is facing something elemental, something ancient, something powerful, something that involves danger and risk.

"The best way to see the canyon is from the bottom," is a saying often quoted. The views from the rims are breathtaking, but only when one looks up from the river—up a mile of sheer wall and steep eroded slopes—can one really see the canyon. Only when riding through the roaring fury of a major rapid can one understand how the canyon came to be. Water against stone; water laden with sand grains, pebbles, and boulders, slowly and steadily, year after year, century after century, finds a path through the canyon.

At night, when the rafters are camped on a sandbar under the stars, the whole universe seems to fit into one great, majestic plan. The canyon has a spell and a mystery all its own and only from deep down, beside or on the Colorado, can these wonders be fully appreciated.

What is it like to ride a raft through the rapids? At first the river flows smooth and calm, but from ahead there sounds an ever-increasing roar. The raft picks up speed. Everyone on board braces feet against the curving pontoon sides and takes a good hard grip on the safety ropes. More speed, louder roar, white water ahead. Then, with a breath-taking plunge, the raft is in the rapids. Spray flies. The bow rises, the raft bends in the middle and the stern is low. Then the stern rises and the bow goes under in a wash. A great wave sweeps over and everybody gets drenched. The raft writhes and tosses while the steersman fights to keep it away from house-sized rocks and from "holes" equally as large and having the potential to keep or flip a raft. Sometimes it is better to hug the shore, to sweep close to sheer walls or a gravelly bar; sometimes it is better to stay in the middle. It all depends on the river channel and the knowledge and skill of the pilot.

On the raft plunges. Seconds lengthen into minutes—the time seems forever—and then the water is calm again. The raft runs ashore and the people pile off, eager to watch the next raft challenge the same caldron. Most people also take pictures. Sometimes, if the rapid is an especially bad one, the less-rugged riders are put ashore first so they can walk past the rapid and watch the raft come through.

The river guides are trained for the job and licensed by the park department. For passenger and raft safety, the guide always "reads" or studies a rapid before running it because, as the current changes, a comparatively gentle rapid on one trip can become a terror on another.

Between rapids, the river flows smoothly; its average speed is about four miles per hour. There are wide places where it is slow and gentle, as though resting up before taking another plunge. The rafts can drift with the current and the riders can study the geology timetable in the canyon walls. There is time to go ashore and explore some of the side canyons and, if conditions are right, enjoy a dip under a waterfall. There are Indian ruins on ledges above the river and these too can be explored.

It is the rapids that make the trip memorable for most people, and it has been so for more than a hundred years. In his book *A Canyon Voyage,* Frederick Dellenbaugh describes running a rapid with these words:

> Nearer and nearer came the angry tumult . . . there was a sudden dropping away of all support; then the mighty waves smote us. . . . The boat rolled and pitched like a ship in a tornado, and as she flew along . . . I could look up under the canopies of foam pouring over gigantic black boulders, first on one side, then on the other. Why we didn't land on top of one of these and turn over I don't know, unless it might be that the very fury of the current causes a recoil. However that may be, we struck nothing but the waves, the boats riding finely and certainly leaping at times almost half their length out of water, to bury themselves quite as far at the next lunge. If you will take a watch and count by it ninety seconds, you will probably have about the time we were in this chaos, though it seemed much longer to me. Then we were through, and immediately took advantage of an eddy on one side to lie to and bail out, for the boat was full of water.

The Colorado that Dellenbaugh experienced was quite different from the Colorado of today. The great river has been tamed by dams and its flow through the canyon is regulated by the amount of water released from Glen Canyon Dam. However, this can vary, depending on the season and the amount of rainfall or snow melt, from as little as 3,000 cubic feet per second (cfs) to as much as 32,000 cfs. The average is about 28,000 cfs. In the B.D. (before dam) period, prior to 1964 when the gates at Glen Canyon Dam were first closed, the Colorado idled along at volumes as low as 700 cfs or roared to the all-time high of 300,000 cfs estimated during a mid-summer flood in 1884. Because of power demands, more water is released during the day than at night, and boaters must keep this in mind when camping on sandbars along the river.

At rare intervals now, when unusually heavy snow melt in the mountains threatens to exceed dam capacity, as it did in the summer of 1983, even more water is released. This effects river runners to some degree, but is much more disastrous for people who have built homes and businesses on the Colorado's flood plain.

Powell and his men began their historic journey from Green River, Wyoming, and traveled a long way on the Green River before reaching the Colorado. Today there are raft trips available on the Green River, but Lake Powell above Glen Canyon Dam has flooded some of the canyons that Powell explored.

Grand Canyon rafters usually "put in" the river at Lee's Ferry, Arizona. From there they can travel all the way to Lake Mead behind Hoover Dam and "take out" at Temple Bar. The motorized trip takes seven to ten days, depending on how many hikes and side trips are included. A rafter can cut the trip in half by leaving the river at Phantom Ranch and taking the trail out, to either the north or south rim. New arrivals can join the rafts at Phantom Ranch and ride the river to Lake Mead.

There are about seventy major rapids in the canyon and each has been rated according to degree of difficulty and danger on a scale of 1 to 10, with 10 representing the most difficult. The rating varies two or three notches up or down, depending on the flow of water. Low water does not necessarily make running the rapid less dangerous. In fact, some rapids are harder to run at low water because there are more rocks to avoid than when the river is higher. On the other hand, too much water may wipe out a rapid entirely for then the water can flow on smoothly well above the rocks.

Local conditions can have drastic results as well. For example, Crystal Rapid, rated between a class 7 and class 10, was created overnight in 1966 by a flash flood that swept down Crystal Creek and washed enough big boulders into the river to make a formidable stretch of rough water.

Each rapid is named. Some are named for people, like President Harding Rapid, so named because the mapping crew stopped there on the day of Harding's funeral in 1923, or Hance Rapid, named for the tall-tale teller who had a riverside cabin nearby. Nankoweap and Shinumo are Indian names; Sapphire and Turquoise rapids are named for the colorful side canyons responsible for them. There are numbered rapids like 110 Mile and 164 Mile rapids, indicating their distance from Lee's Ferry. Upset Rapid recalls a boating mishap, and Sockdolager is named from 19th-century slang.

Badger Creek and Soap Creek, both of which empty into dangerous rapids with the same names, have an interesting story attached to their naming. It seems that Jacob Hamblin, the Mormon explorer who is known as the Buckskin Apostle, killed a badger on one creek and carried it to his camp on the other creek. He skinned the animal and put it in a pot over the fire to boil all night. Next morning, to his surprise, he found that the alkali in the creek water and the fat in the badger had combined to turn his stew into soap—a most unappetizing breakfast.

River Rats take rough water as it comes, hanging on and enjoying the thrill that each rapid brings. There are occasional accidents, usually the result of recklessness or carelessness. Boating safety regulations require everyone to wear a life jacket at all times when riding the rafts and, because each rapid means another wetting, rafters and life jackets stay damp most of the time. The bane of every rafter's existence is having to put on a wet, cold life jacket at the start of each day.

Because the Colorado is muddy, rafters get muddy, too. That is why they welcome the clear side streams and waterfalls that sometimes provide a clean bath or shower. Hair is gritty, whiskers grow in a muddy stubble, clothes and shoes stay damp and get rather gamy. For these reasons, at the end of the ride, a hot bath is the most welcome feature of "civilization." Perhaps that is also why a sign on the truck that picks up Georgie White's Royal River Rats once read:

"Old River Rats never die—They just smell that way."

As the years have passed, the question increasingly arises: Are raft trips a good thing or a bad thing for river ecology? River Rats have become far too numerous, some preservationists maintain, and the ever-increasing raft traffic is taking its toll on the canyon. No longer can the mighty Colorado flush itself out periodically with high water and floods; the dam has stopped that. But even though people are required to carry out everything they bring into the canyon (including the contents of their portable toilets), camping places and the environment in general have begun to deteriorate.

The summer of 1983 was an exception. Because of extremely high runoff from snowmelt in the mountains, great quantities of water had to be released from Lake Powell and, beyond the canyon, from Lake Mead. The flood rushed through the canyon and scoured the sandbars and the camping places, leaving them, in general, better than before. There were some changes—old sandbars gone and new ones of fresh, clean sand created. River runners were pleased, although people farther downstream were flooded and unhappy.

In an effort to protect canyon ecology, the park department now limits the number of rafts and expeditions that river outfitters can offer each year. Oar-powered raft trips are encouraged and, to please people who resent the sound of motors in the canyon, there are times when only the splash of oars can be heard. At other times, the larger rafts and their motors still ride the river.

Extreme environmentalists would prefer to have river trips banned entirely and the whole region declared a wilderness area, but this is a bit drastic. Perhaps, in future years *Homo sapiens riverensis* will be less numerous—an endangered species, possibly. But it is doubtful that they will ever follow some other canyon creatures into extinction.

The floppy-eared burro was brought to the canyon as a beast of burden. When their services were no longer needed, the burros were abandoned in the canyon, where they continued to thrive and reproduce.

CHAPTER IX

BURRO TALES

SOMETIMES THERE CAN BE TOO MUCH OF A GOOD THING. BURROS IN THE GRAND Canyon are a good example of this old saying. When the West was young and people needed a dependable beast of burden, the burro was a very good thing. But years passed and conditions changed. Prospectors stopped prospecting, trails became roads, miners used trains, trucks, jeeps and even airplanes to carry themselves and their ores to market. Burros were no longer needed, so the long-eared creatures were turned loose to shift for themselves. Burros were good at that. They ran free, went wild, and increased in numbers until they were no longer a good thing. Instead, they became a definite problem, especially in some of the national parks and monuments. But to start at the beginning. . . .

Burros, like horses, are recent immigrants to the Western Hemisphere. Their ancestors once lived in this part of the world but became extinct here thousands of years ago. Their descendants survived in parts of Africa and Asia, and it was in these regions that both the burro and the horse were first domesticated. Centuries passed. Finally, both the burro and the horse returned to the lands of their ancestors along with the Spanish conquistadores. Horses and asses (the burro is an ass) were among the first animals brought by Columbus for the colonies he founded in the New World. The horse came as human transportation; the burro came to carry whatever else needed carrying.

Later, when prospectors began searching the West for minerals and other wealth, the burro again carried the loads. A prospector and his burro were a team that could go on for months at a time, far from anything resembling civilization. Then, if the prospector did manage to strike it rich, it was again the burro, or whole pack trains of burros, that carried the ore to market.

Not every prospector found a bonanza—in fact, mighty few of them did, especially in the Grand Canyon area. Some finally gave up in disgust, went searching in other places, or even got steady jobs. Some died in the field and the coyotes picked their bones. Some just disappeared and were never heard from again. A few burros probably wandered away and left their owners to make it back to civilization as best they could, but in most cases it was the human who abandoned the burro. A few old-time residents purposely turned burros loose in the canyon so there would always be a supply of load carriers available. It was cheaper to let the burros breed and care for themselves than it was to feed and look after them until they might be needed.

The burro, being an intelligent and adaptable creature (the burro is not a stupid ass) proceeded to thrive and multiply. He found the sparse canyon vegetation to his liking—his teeth were good enough to chew it and his stomach juices strong enough to digest it. He had an uncanny ability to smell out springs and water holes, and his tough little hoofs could dig in damp places for water if need be. Like the camel, a burro can go longer without water than most other animals.

Burros live about twenty-five years (some domesticated ones have been known to live up to forty or fifty years), and a female burro (she is called a jenny while the male is called a jack) has a foal every year during most of her life. Baby burros are hardy youngsters; there is little infant mortality among them, their mothers take good care of them, and they have no natural enemies. In other times and places, burros provided food for lions, leopards, tigers, wolves, and even humans. But the big beasts of prey are long gone from the canyon, and there is no human market for burro steaks or burro burgers.

Consequently, from the turn of the century through the 1920s, the "wild" burros multiplied in Grand Canyon National Park and became a real problem. The trouble was that they took over the food, water, and living areas of native animals, especially the desert bighorn sheep, which were becoming increasingly scarce. This caused a lot of headaches because government agencies were required by law to protect and preserve the native animals. During the 1920s, burro hunts were held in the park, and rangers and other official hunters armed with high powered rifles killed more than 1400 burros. This, they thought, had solved the burro problem.

The general public was not aware of the problem nor of its solution; in fact, they were charmed by the burro—shaggy, big-eared, sad-eyed, pint-sized, picturesque, a symbol of the Old West that everybody loved and admired.

One burro in particular won the public's heart and in the process symbolized all the other burros roaming free in the Grand Canyon. His name was Brighty and he was known as the "hermit of Bright Angel Creek." He was first encountered in 1892 when a couple of cowboys found the full-grown animal grazing near an abandoned tent on the Kaibab Plateau. What had become of his original owner was never known and, since there was no one to claim him, Brighty never had another permanent owner.

From time to time he was caught and put to work; he carried materials, equipment, and supplies for the crew that built the first suspension bridge across the Colorado and was given the honor of being the first to cross it when completed. Winters he spent in the lower part of the canyon, but in spring he worked his way to the north rim and for six years he carried water for the National Park Service there. He liked to be petted and allowed children to ride him, yet he never gave up his wild freedom during the thirty years he lived in canyon country.

Brighty disappeared from the scene about 1922. Legend says that he was killed and eaten by a couple of outlaws hiding for the winter on the north rim. He must have been pretty old and tough by that time.

The memory of Brighty lingered and was brought back to national (and international) fame in 1953 in an award-winning children's book, *Brighty of the Grand Canyon,* written by Marguerite Henry. The story of Brighty was made into a motion picture, with a burro from Illinois named Jiggs playing the lead role.

A life-sized, brass statue of Brighty was, for a time, proudly displayed on the north rim. But as the burro problem grew serious, the statue was moved to a less conspicuous place in the downstairs lobby of the Grand Canyon Lodge. It is there today; its nose is bright and shiny from all the rubs that visitors give it, just for luck.

Meanwhile, after the hunts ended, the remaining burros continued to multiply. A few were removed or destroyed from time to time, but the public disapproved, especially of the destruction. By 1976, there were an estimated three thousand wild burros in the Grand Canyon. They were devouring the vegetation, fouling the water holes, increasing erosion by wearing away trails, and destroying archaeological sites by rubbing against the walls and trampling the ruins. Besides this, they were taking over bighorn grazing grounds, pushing the native animals out. The bighorn population was already endangered. The burros definitely were not.

Land management people argued that the burros were not native to the canyon, did not belong there, and certainly were not an endangered species. The canyon, they said, could support a maximum of only 178 burros—no more than one animal for every ten square miles of suitable land. The others would have to go.

But then three national animal protection organizations stepped into the act. They protested loudly and one of them, the New York based Fund for the Animals, agreed to put up a quarter of a million dollars to airlift the burros out of the canyon and place them in approved homes. The native bighorn sheep are shy creatures; their plight did not get much publicity.

So the burros were to be saved, but first they had to be caught. Six cowboys from Wickiup, Arizona, with twenty-one horses and six cowdogs went in to do the job in the summer of 1981. There were television and movie crews on hand to watch, along with a goodly number of newspaper reporters. Burros were rounded up and kept in holding pens near the base camp (they were not segregated by sex so many more burritos were created) until, one by one, they were airlifted by helicopter to a corral on the rim. Television viewers all over the country saw the burros ride out in cargo nets dangling beneath a helicopter with the Grand Canyon in the background. When the process was over, tons of trash and human litter also had to be removed from the area.

The exact number of burros removed is not known, but each was removed at a cost of about two thousand dollars, and the Fund for the Animals reportedly spent over one million dollars on the program; they received lots of publicity in the process.

But professional wildlife management people groaned and growled at the cost, pointing out that no burro so "rescued" would live more than twenty years and that removal would add nothing to the general ecology. The money could have been spent much more wisely and effectively, they said, for the benefit of native wildlife. In a more practical vein, it was also pointed out that burros could be shot and permanently removed for sixty dollars per animal, or herded out of the canyon for about $440 per burro. But that would not have given the television crews anything to photograph.

The burro problem is not the Grand Canyon's exclusive headache. Bandalier and Death Valley national monuments plus other federal lands must deal with the same situation. In an effort to find homes for the animals, the U.S. Department of Interior's Bureau of Land Management has set up an "adopt a wild horse or burro program," whereby individuals can apply to adopt as many as four animals per year. Kingman, Arizona, is the adoption center nearest the Grand Canyon.

Adoptors must agree to give the adoptees proper care and handling. The adoption agreement specifically states that the animals can be trained for riding, working, showing, packing, or any other purpose for which the domesticated horse or burro can be used; they cannot be used for bucking stock, or anything that would exploit their wildness, for at least a year. During that year, the animal is still the property of the U.S. government. After a year, the adoptor can apply for ownership. Then, with certification of humane treatment from a veterinarian and approval from the BLM, the adoptor is given a certificate of title for the adoptee.

Author Marguerite Henry touched the heartstrings of animal lovers and western romantics when she ended *Brighty of the Grand Canyon* with these words:

> Some animals, like some men, leave a trail of glory behind them. They give their spirit to the place where they have lived, and remain forever a part of the rocks and streams and the wind and sky.
>
> Especially on moonlit nights a shaggy little form can be seen flirting along the ledges, a thin swirl of dust rising behind him. But the older guides swear it is a trail out of the past, kicked up by Brighty himself, the roving spirit of the Grand Canyon—forever wild, forever free.

Poor Brighty and his many relatives. They have been too successful in the Grand Canyon. In their case, success has not paid off in the long run.

THERE ARE MANY FACTS AND FEATURES TO BE FOUND IN THE GRAND CANYON. EVEN though they are true, some of them are less easy to accept than many of the tall tales. But accept them we must because they can be proven by figures, by measurements, and by scientific observations. Of course, no humans were around two billion years ago when the region was in the process of formation, and no one was around even ten million years ago when the canyon first began to take form. But geologists are accepted authorities and no one questions their reading of the canyon's tremendous timetable.

To mere people whose life spans are measured in a few decades, the great stretch of time recorded by layers of rock in the canyon is hard to believe. Yet scientists tell us that as we hike down any trail we can read the record of ages, from the present back through millions of years. We can see the remains of ancient sea beds and deserts, of mountains that were pushed up and eroded away, of volcanoes that lived, spewed lava, died and disappeared. The same is true for ancient life forms that crawled, swam, flew, or ran, and ancient plants that grew in this region long, long before the creature called *Homo sapiens* was ever thought of.

Fortunately, there are many truths about the canyon that we can understand, even though we may again be hard put to believe them. Consider, for example, the Colorado River that is responsible for the Grand Canyon. Scientists tell us that the river has always flowed at about the same elevation; it is the land that has risen and not the river. Slowly, of course, the earth pushed itself up. Meanwhile, the river flowed steadily along, keeping its bed constant by wearing it away at the same pace that the region rose.

Standing on the south rim and looking down at the brown thread of water far below (there are not many places on the north rim from which the river is visible) the viewer finds the river's size and strength hard to believe. Only the Mississippi, Missouri, and Rio Grande rivers are longer than the Colorado and its main tributary, the Green. The Colorado River system drains an area of more than 240,000 square miles, or nearly one-twelfth of the United States. It flows through nineteen major canyons as it drops from its origin 10,000 feet up in the Rocky Mountains to sea level where it empties into the Gulf of California (also called the Sea of Cortez). Its current forms about 365 rapids, seventy of which are within the Grand Canyon.

A river of such dimensions is worthy of respect. As Barry Goldwater wrote after a boat trip through the canyon in 1940, "It is wiser to tip your hat to this stream than to thumb your nose at it."

There are many other true stories about the canyon that may be recorded. No book can possibly relate them all. Looking ahead, down through the years, it is interesting to speculate on what changes the future will bring. Certainly in the foreseeable future—the next million or so years—the river will continue to flow, the lakes behind the dams will fill up with silt, *Homo sapiens* may or may not become an endangered species. If it took ten million years for the Grand Canyon to develop, who knows what tall tales and true details the next ten million years will bring.